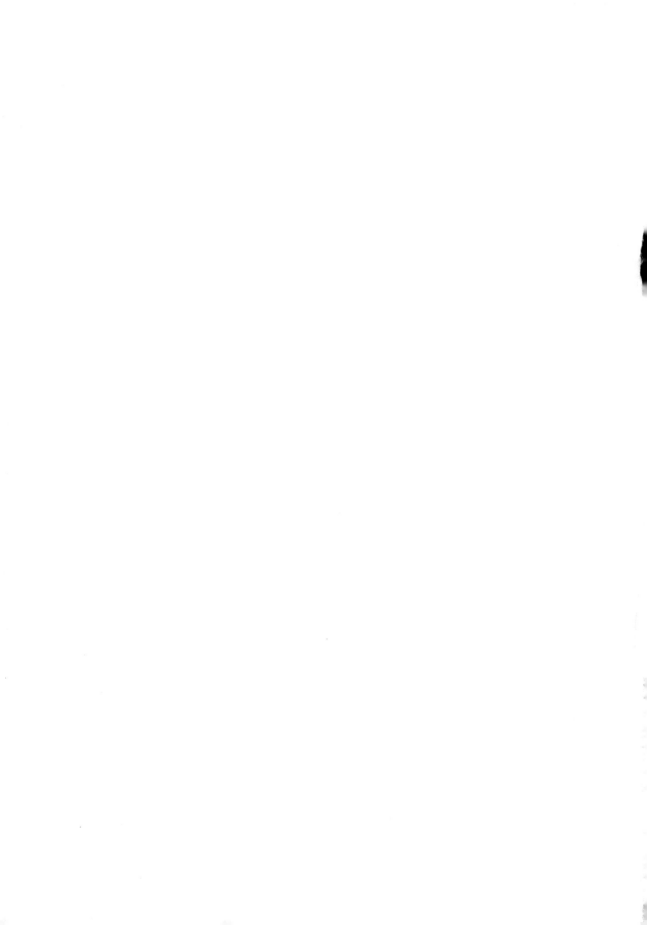

Beginning Salesforce Developer

Michael Wicherski

Apress®

Beginning Salesforce Developer

Michael Wicherski
Los Angeles, California, USA

ISBN-13 (pbk): 978-1-4842-3299-6   ISBN-13 (electronic): 978-1-4842-3300-9
https://doi.org/10.1007/978-1-4842-3300-9

Library of Congress Control Number: 2017962310

Cover image by Freepik (www.freepik.com)

Managing Director: Welmoed Spahr
Editorial Director: Todd Green
Acquisitions Editor: Susan McDermott
Development Editor: Laura Berendson
Technical Reviewer: Haulson Wong
Coordinating Editor: Rita Fernando
Copy Editor: Brendan Frost

Distributed to the book trade worldwide by Springer Science+Business Media New York, 233 Spring Street, 6th Floor, New York, NY 10013. Phone 1-800-SPRINGER, fax (201) 348-4505, e-mail orders-ny@springer-sbm.com, or visit www.springeronline.com. Apress Media, LLC is a California LLC and the sole member (owner) is Springer Science + Business Media Finance Inc (SSBM Finance Inc). SSBM Finance Inc is a **Delaware** corporation.

For information on translations, please e-mail rights@apress.com, or visit http://www.apress.com/rights-permissions.

Apress titles may be purchased in bulk for academic, corporate, or promotional use. eBook versions and licenses are also available for most titles. For more information, reference our Print and eBook Bulk Sales web page at http://www.apress.com/bulk-sales.

Any source code or other supplementary material referenced by the author in this book is available to readers on GitHub via the book's product page, located at www.apress.com/9781484232996. For more detailed information, please visit http://www.apress.com/source-code.

Printed on acid-free paper

For my dad, who only ever asked that I try my best.

Table of Contents

About the Author

Dennis Sheppard is the VP of Technology at NextTier Education, a startup dedicated to helping students navigate the college selection process. Long before that, though, Dennis graduated from Louisiana Tech University with a computer science degree and went on to develop and architect software for almost a dozen different industries. With over 10 years of professional software development experience, he has built his share of web applications, for both mobile and desktop. Because of that, Dennis strongly believes in the power of Progressive Web Apps to further help the tech world reach those who don't have access to the fastest networks and latest and greatest phones. He was born and raised in the Deep South, but migrated to the suburbs of Chicago where he lives with his wife, a set of twins who are growing up way too fast, and an arthritic but playful golden retriever.

About the Technical Reviewer

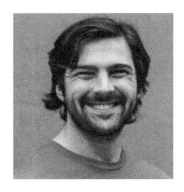

Phil Nash is a developer evangelist for Twilio and a Google Developer Expert. He's been in the web industry for 10 years building with JavaScript, Ruby, and Swift. He can be found hanging out at meetups and conferences, playing with new technologies and APIs, or writing open source code online. Sometimes he makes his own beer, but he's more likely to be found discovering new ones around the world.

Phil tweets at @philnash and you can find him elsewhere online at `https://philna.sh`.

Acknowledgments

I think everyone who has ever written a book has at least a little bit of crazy in them. Because of that, there needs to a handful of people to help manage the crazy. I'm particularly lucky to have a lot of people to help me with that. Without these people, what you're about to read would be a much bigger mess than it already is.

First, a huge thank you to Brooke McEntee for creating the diagrams and icons in the book. She did a miraculous job transforming my awful sketches into what you see here. If any part of the diagrams isn't perfect, that's 100% on me.

Thank you to my friend and coworker Carly Kaluzna for her encouragement and for coming up with the name iPatch, so you can blame her for that. Thank you to my former co-author AJ Liptak whom I constantly bounce ideas off and ask technical questions that I could just as easily google. Thanks to Becky Lehmann for helping me to be a better teacher and urging me to continue with unparalleled positivity. Thanks to Rick Williams for being ready to celebrate with me as soon as this book is finished. Thank you to Justin Shiffman who always champions whatever I'm working on, even if he did say he'd pay me not to write another book. Thank you to Dave Hoag who first introduced me to PWAs a couple of years ago, and thank you to the entire NextTier team, who will have a new addition to the book-stack monitor stands.

Thank you to the team at Apress: Joan Murray, Jill Balzano, and Laura Berendson, as well as the book's technical reviewer, Phil Nash.

Thanks to Addy Osmani, Jake Archibald, John Papa, and many others in the PWA dev community. We've never met, but you'll never know how much you've taught me.

Thank you to my family for instilling in me a love of books growing up. Thank you to Violet, Cameron, and Betsy Sheppard for always inspiring and motivating me.

And finally, thank you, Reader. With all of the videos and blogs and tutorials available on the Internet today, a tech book isn't always an easy purchase. Thank you for having faith. I hope you learn a lot and have a little bit of fun.

A note on the use of certain images: the browser icons used in Chapter 1 were designed by Pixel Buddha from Flaticon, the iPatch app's pirate icon first introduced in Chapter 6 was created by freedesignfile.com, and Peggy the Parrot's image first introduced in Chapter 7 was created by Freepik.

PART I

Intro to PWAs and Tooling

CHAPTER 1

Introduction to Progressive Web Apps

When was the last time you visited an app's mobile web site rather than its native app counterpart? Was it an enjoyable experience? What did you like about it? What could have been better?

Possibly one of the things you liked was the convenience. You didn't have to go to an app store to download the app and you didn't have to worry about the app being unavailable for your particular phone. You weren't forced to install anything to clutter up your phone's home screen with another app icon.

Was there anything you didn't like? Was the web app slower to load than you would've liked? If you didn't have a solid 4G Internet connection, data might not have displayed quickly or correctly. Maybe you would've liked to receive notifications of an alert in the app. Perhaps you don't mind the home screen clutter and would have liked the option to save the app to your home screen so you wouldn't have to type in the URL again next time.

For most mobile web sites you visit today, these are some of the tradeoffs you have to make. The Web has significant reach; no need for the latest iPhone just to get content. From your grandma's 10-year-old computer to a five-year-old Android tablet to the most cutting edge phone, the Web is everywhere. No one can deny its reach. Unfortunately, depending on your Internet connection, it can be slow and clunky.

Over time, there have been improvements. Processors got faster, browsers got smarter, and blog posts about performance tips and tricks are only a Google search away. Unfortunately, though, all of that wasn't enough. The Web could still be slow on poor connections. Sites had no way to notify you of something going on in the app. And the idea of a web app working with little or no connectivity was crazy. It seemed like after all was said and done, native apps were not only a clear winner, but really the only logical choice for app developers. In fact, a 2015 report from comScore noted that

© Dennis Sheppard 2017
D. Sheppard, *Beginning Progressive Web App Development*, https://doi.org/10.1007/978-1-4842-3090-9_1

smartphone users spend 87 percent of their time in apps (`www.comscore.com/Insights/Presentations-and-Whitepapers/2016/The-2016-US-Mobile-App-Report`); see Figure 1-1.

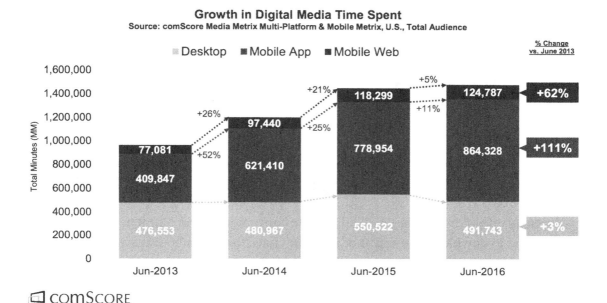

Figure 1-1.   *Apps take up all our time, according to comScore*

Yikes! What are you doing reading a book about web apps, then? Let's learn about Swift and Kotlin! Well, don't ditch this book just yet! It's true that users love their apps. The deepest engagement is in apps. But good luck getting that level of engagement. Another 2015 report, this time Forrester's US Consumer Technographics Behavioral Study from October 2014 to December 2014, noted that smartphone users spend 84 percent of that time in five apps. It's a different top five for most users, but unless you're Facebook, Snapchat, Instagram, or Google, there is a great chance you aren't cracking that top five. Back away from the Swift book!

In fact, because most users cling tightly to their favorite five apps, mobile web actually gets more eyeballs than apps do, as you can see in Figure 1-2.

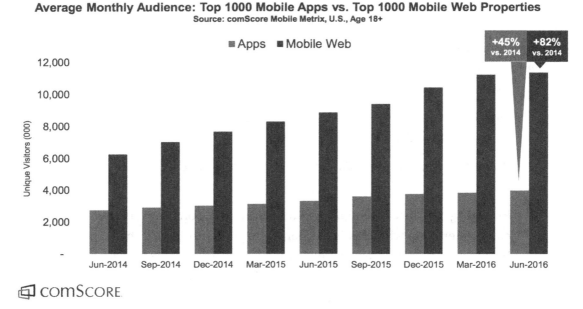

Figure 1-2. *But mobile web takes up all our eyeballs, according to comScore*

After the most popular apps, there's a steep drop off of mobile app usage. So if you're producing the 912th most visited mobile web site, you're going to get around three times more visitors than if you're producing the 912th most used mobile web app. That is significant. No one can doubt the Web's vast reach.

So what does this mean for those of us who aren't developing for billion dollar companies (or at least those of us who aren't developing for billion dollar companies that produce a user's top five apps)? It means that the little bit of user's time we can capture on the Web had better be **good**.

And that's where Progressive Web Apps swoop in to save the day.

What a Progressive Web App Actually Is

Let's forget about simply visiting a web app for a moment. Have you ever tried to build a mobile web app? Did it perform as well as you would've liked? Did you try it on a really old Android phone? Were you able to alert your users of new content or a new message from your app? Unless you had the opportunity to implement features of Progressive Web Apps, it's possible that your users had a suboptimal experience.

Progressive Web Apps aren't built using a singular, specific technology. They're not a new framework, and they're not a new language. Instead, PWAs are a set of strategies, techniques, and APIs that allow developers to give users the native mobile-like experience they're used to.

Progressive Web Apps are

- **Fast**, often rendering something on the user's device in less than a couple of seconds.

- **Reliable**, even without a solid data connection, and even on old devices.

- **Engaging**, because by enabling notifications, even on the Web, users can be alerted to whatever is happening in your app, even if the browser isn't open. Users can even install a Progressive Web App right to their phone's home screen. Developers can choose the icon and even set up a splash screen.

Possibly the best part of Progressive Web Apps, though, is inherent to the platform: their reach. There are 6.4 **BILLION** devices connected to the Internet. That's a lot of devices, and a lot of reach. You don't need to learn Objective-C or Swift or Java or Kotlin to reach every one of those 6.4 billion devices. You can use the tools you likely already know: HTML, CSS, and JavaScript.

So now let's get down to the nuts and bolts of what makes up a Progressive Web App.

A Progressive Web App, first and foremost, works everywhere. Even if it's a small subset of features, to be a true PWA, your app needs to have some kind of functionality on the most basic device. Maybe it's just a static page that shows up on a five-year-old Android phone. But it works. It's not just a blank screen or a bunch of error messages.

As your user's browser gets more modern, more features become available to your user. This is known as *progressive enhancement*. Figure 1-3 shows that the same code that displays as a plain website grows into a powerful application as browser support improves. That's where the true power of PWAs comes in: your users' experiences get progressively better as their browsers get better. The experience improves via a collection of features that gives your app depth to engage users, reliability regardless of the quality of the Internet connection, and enough speed so that it doesn't make anyone wait around for your content to load. I'll cover each of those features in depth later on, but so that you're not left hanging, let's talk about a few of them at a high level.

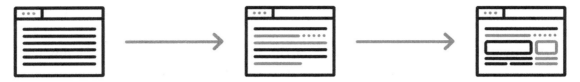

Figure 1-3. *Progressive enhancement*

Offline support: The main page of your app loads even while the user is offline. This is accomplished with *service workers*. I'll show how to use service workers to accomplish what you see in Figure 1-4: how to cache your app's assets so that even if your users don't have the best Internet connection (or a connection at all), they still get to soak in your sweet, sweet content.

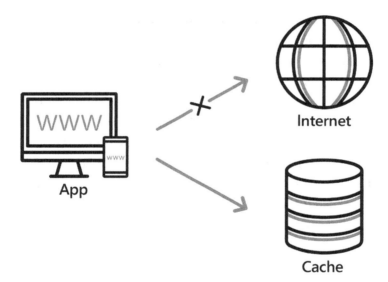

Figure 1-4. *Offline support via caching*

Performance: (Yes, performance absolutely is a feature!) The app's first page load is fast, even on slow 3G connections. There are a few things I'll cover that go into making that a reality, but an important one is having an *app shell*. I'll go over creating an app shell that renders almost instantly while the rest of your app is loading. Another important feature for performance is *web workers* that allow you to make other parts of your app do the heavy processing that would normally slow down your UI.

Home screen icon and a splash screen: Your app can be added to the user's home screen so they don't have to navigate to a URL every time they want to use your app. And at the app's launch, instead of a blank white screen while your app is loading, you can

have a splash screen just like those fancy native apps. You'll use the *app manifest* to take care of all that.

Notifications: If there's anything going on in your app that the user should know about while they're not actively using it, the app can notify them with *push notifications*. I'll cover the web notifications and the Push API so you can remind your users about that aforementioned content.

Current and Future PWA Support

PWAs are exciting. But let's throw in a little dose of reality. One of the biggest downsides of the Web that has been a struggle since the beginning of time is browser support. Ugh, browsers. There are so many, and each one doesn't always support the latest and greatest awesome technology. Alas, such is the case for PWAs. Remember, though, one of the most important tenets of PWAs is that they should provide a progressively better experience for your users as their browsers' capabilities increase. So just because a browser doesn't support a feature you're really looking forward to implementing doesn't mean you should abandon all hope, nor does it mean that the browser might not support it in the future. Plus, if a user is checking out your app on a browser that does support most or all PWA features, that user is in for an excellent World Wide Web experience.

For the most part, we'll be focusing on five major browsers: Chrome, Safari, Firefox, Opera, and Edge. Because PWAs are such a focus of Google's lately, it should come as no surprise that, as you can see in Figure 1-5, Chrome has the most robust support for every PWA feature, followed by Firefox and Opera, with Safari and Edge trailing the others fairly significantly in their support.

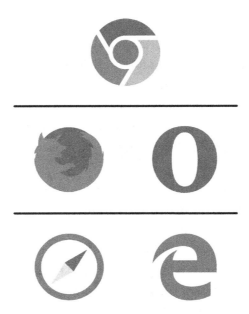

Figure 1-5. *Browser PWA support hierarchy*

Note   There are other browsers that have solid usage, depending on where in the world you live. A couple of the more popular ones are UC Browser, which is widely used in Asia, and Samsung Internet Browser, which has a large share of the market in Europe. Both have solid PWA support that's almost on par with Chrome.

Let's go over some of the individual features we've talked about and look at their current support.

Service workers: On the desktop, Chrome fully supports service workers and has had some level of support since early 2015. The same goes for Firefox and Opera. As of mid-2017, Edge supported service workers, but not by default; they had to be enabled via a setting in the browser. As of Edge 16, however, they're enabled by default. In a great coup for PWAs and service worker domination, Safari announced in August of 2017 that service worker support was under development. By the time you're reading this, Safari should (hopefully) support service workers like a boss. On the mobile side, the story is similar. Android supports service workers through Chrome, while iOS has no service worker support right now, but it is on the way!

Web workers: Web workers have the best browser support of just about any PWA feature. Every major browser fully supports web workers on both desktop and mobile.

Push API and Notification API: The story here is similar to service workers. On the desktop, Chrome, Firefox, and Opera all support both the Push API and web notifications (I'll dive into the differences in Chapter 6). While Safari supports web notifications, it has a custom implementation for push notifications. Edge supports web notifications, but has no Push API support. On the mobile side, iOS has no support for either feature, while Android supports just the Push API.

Web app manifest: Again, Chrome and Opera come out as clear winners here. The app manifest is supported in those two browsers and on Android. Unfortunately, no other browsers support the app manifest, yet. Edge and Firefox, however, are currently working on implementing support, and as of mid-2017, Firefox did support a handful of web app manifest features. Safari is taking the web app manifest under consideration.

IndexedDB: Almost every major browser supports IndexedDB on both desktop and mobile browsers. The lone exception is Edge, which has partial support.

Please keep in mind that support for these technologies will only improve (until something better comes along). So if you're reading this far into the future, do a little research to see if a particular feature is supported in different browsers. The Mozilla Developer Network and `www.caniuse.com` are both great resources to find out what web features are compatible with various browser versions.

Looking Ahead

In this book, you'll learn how to implement all these features (and others) to make your web apps super powered. Along the way, you'll learn how to measure your app to make sure it's not missing any PWA features that could take your app to the next level. And once you've learned all of that, you're going to take a real-world "traditional" application and turn it into a blazing fast PWA with all of your newfound knowledge. If you're a React dev or you're an Angular dev (no framework wars, please!), you're covered there, too. I'll go over how to start off on the right foot with your new app built in a lot of the most popular JS frameworks around today. Then, in case your app needs just one more extra nudge, I'll go over a few more essential performance items that will really help your users forget about native apps. Let's get started!

CHAPTER 2

Tools to Measure Progressive Web Apps

Before you go too far down the path of learning how to implement PWA features, it may help to know exactly what goals you're trying to achieve, and how to measure your apps against those goals. I've already mentioned the core principles of Progressive Web Apps, but there are a lot of other little things I haven't touched on. Most of them wouldn't warrant a discussion all on their own; they're just simple things you should do to make your app all it can be.

How do you know what those little things are? There's a PWA checklist that Google helpfully provides at `https://developers.google.com/web/progressive-web-apps/checklist`. This is a great list of goals, and even breaks them up into "Baseline" and "Exemplary" goals. Reading this list will give you a good idea of what you can do as a developer to build really great web apps. Even better, though, would be if you could see certain sites in action and easily compare them to your list of goals to see if even big-name sites can cross everything off that list. This is where Lighthouse comes in.

A Light to Keep You Off the Rocks

Google's Lighthouse tool evaluates a site to see how well it complies with Progressive Web App principles. There are three ways to use Lighthouse: through the CLI, via the *Audit* tab in Chrome DevTools, and through the Chrome plugin. Let's go through the plugin installation as well as the process to run a report in DevTools to see exactly what you can measure.

To install the plugin, open Chrome and go to the Chrome Web Store and search for Lighthouse (or simply search Google for Chrome Lighthouse). Install the extension and you should have a new icon in your list of extensions.

© Dennis Sheppard 2017
D. Sheppard, *Beginning Progressive Web App Development*, https://doi.org/10.1007/978-1-4842-3090-9_2

Now, let's navigate to a site. Here we'll look at Reddit.com, but feel free to try something else. Once the site loads, open Lighthouse and you'll see a *Generate a Report* button. Once you click that, you will see what Lighthouse options are available to you, as in Figure 2-1.

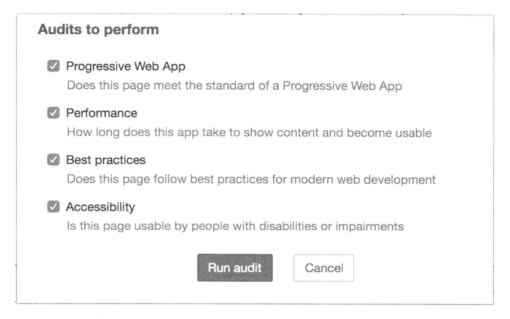

Figure 2-1. *Lighthouse options*

Currently there are four different categories you can ask Lighthouse to test for:

- Progressive Web App

- Performance

- Accessibility

- Best Practices

Leave all of them checked so you're able to see everything Lighthouse tests.

Click the *Generate Report* button. As soon as you do that, Lighthouse is going to start *doing things* to that browser tab. It will resize it and reload it and lots of other things. Let it work for a minute, and soon it will generate a report.

There are a lot of results. Results for Reddit show scores of 45/100 for Progressive Web App, 45/100 for performance, 94/100 for accessibility, and 85/100 for best practices.

I'm not going over each of these results because a) that'd take forever b) you might not be that interested in every one of them and c) the results come with handy

explanations because each item is expandable. Let's take a few minutes to talk about what a few of the most important items are and why they're important. I'll get into fixing any issues with these items throughout the book.

Let's start with the PWA section in Figure 2-2.

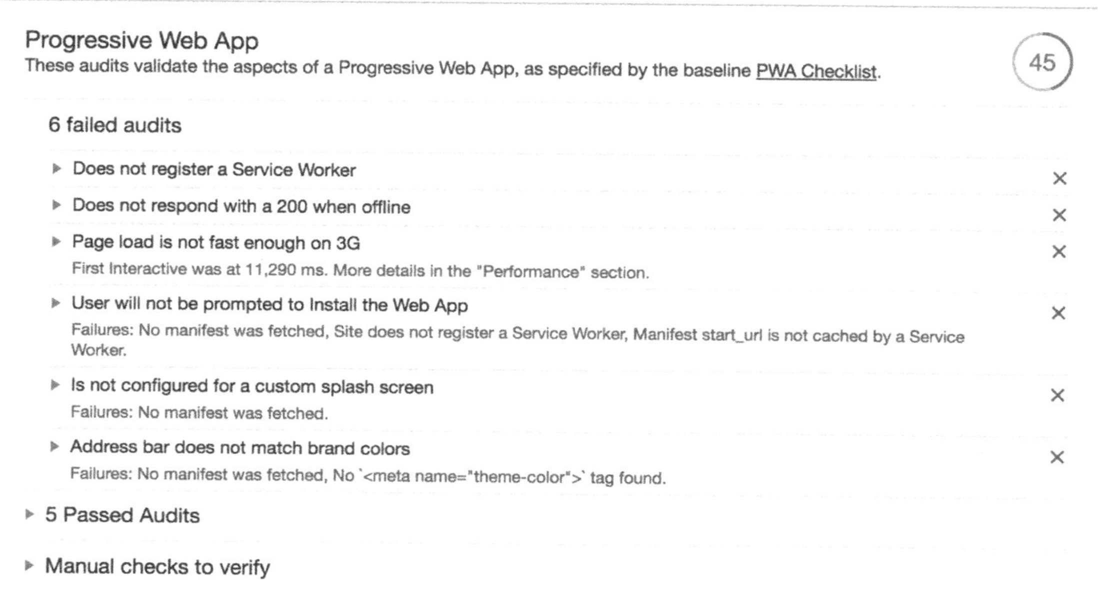

Progressive Web App

These audits validate the aspects of a Progressive Web App, as specified by the baseline <u>PWA Checklist</u>.

(45)

6 failed audits

▶ Does not register a Service Worker ✕

▶ Does not respond with a 200 when offline ✕

▶ Page load is not fast enough on 3G ✕
First Interactive was at 11,290 ms. More details in the "Performance" section.

▶ User will not be prompted to Install the Web App ✕
Failures: No manifest was fetched, Site does not register a Service Worker, Manifest start_url is not cached by a Service Worker.

▶ Is not configured for a custom splash screen ✕
Failures: No manifest was fetched.

▶ Address bar does not match brand colors ✕
Failures: No manifest was fetched, No `<meta name="theme-color">` tag found.

▶ 5 Passed Audits

▶ Manual checks to verify

Figure 2-2. *Lighthouse results: Progressive Web App section*

Here, you can see that Reddit does not register a service worker. Thus, the site won't load anything when you have no connection, and items won't be cached with the Cache API for fast retrieval on subsequent page loads.

Now let's take a look at something Reddit passes, and something I haven't talked about yet. Reddit uses HTTPS. HTTPS is an extremely important security measure for web apps to help prevent malicious attacks. Long gone are the days when only sites that handled financial or medical data and the like needed to secure their apps.

Feel free to explore the other sections of the PWA score for the site you chose. For now, let's move on to the Performance section.

The interesting sections here to note are the *First meaningful paint* and the *First Interactive*. These are the times in which your users see your content for the first time. There are numerous studies showing engagement rates based on how long it takes a site to load. Faster is better. You'll look at various ways to increase your score on this metric, but Lighthouse gives a few suggestions of its own, including reducing the number of

blocking resources. These are resources such as stylesheets or scripts that need to load before your page renders on the screen. That results in a perceived longer load time for your app. Also notice in Figure 2-3 the pretty handy series of screenshots Lighthouse provides of the different loading states of your app.

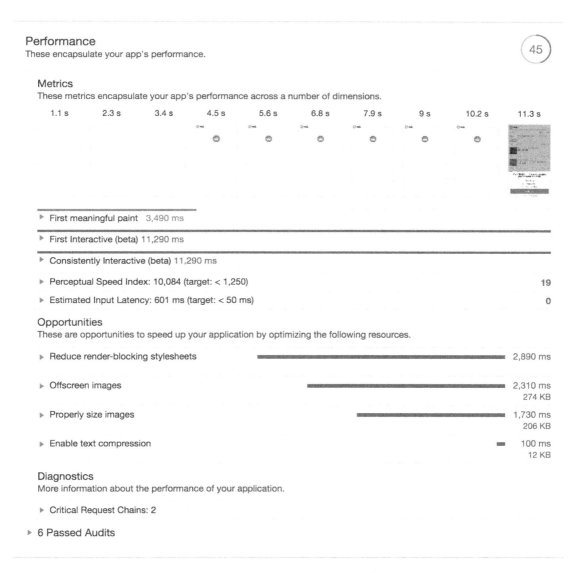

Figure 2-3. *Lighthouse results: Performance section*

Also interesting to note here is *Avoids an excessive DOM size*. The more intricate your app's layout is, the longer it will take to render. Sometimes a complex layout is just inherent to your app's design, but it's something to consider when you're thinking about performance.

Onward to the Accessibility section. Accessibility is a very large topic, and for the most part it's out of the scope of this book. There are many wonderful resources you can seek out to find ways to make your site accessible to anyone. That's what accessibility is all about: ensuring your app's content and functionality is available to anyone who wants it, particularly those with a physical impairment that could otherwise make accessing your app difficult. Take a few minutes to read through this section of Lighthouse and you'll get an idea of what you should keep in mind while developing your application. These aren't difficult guidelines to follow, and most developers simply need to be made aware that they exist in order to implement them.

The last section of the Lighthouse report is Best Practices. Obviously that's a pretty broad term, so let's take a look at some of the metrics. Here you'll find *Uses HTTPS* again just like in the PWA section. Two for the price of one; let's take it. You should also see somewhere in there *Avoids Application Cache* and *Avoids WebSQL DB*. Both of these technologies are deprecated in favor of service workers and IndexedDB, respectively, and I'll cover those newer, better technologies later on. You should take a few moments to read over each of them, but the last one we'll look at together is *Avoids requesting the notification permission on page load*. That's an easy one to pass if your app doesn't have notifications. However, if you do plan on implementing notifications for your app, there are better ways to ask the user for notification permission than blasting them in the face as soon as the app loads. I'll cover more of that in Chapter 7.

That's Lighthouse. Each section has a corresponding explanation and a lot of material to go along with it, provided by Google. It's worth spending some time on each of them, but until you're at a good spot in building your PWA, it might not be that helpful. So for now, let's move on.

Chrome DevTools

Lighthouse is the primary PWA measurement tool, but there are other tools that can help you create better PWAs. A big one is Chrome DevTools. Browser developer tools have come a long way since the Firebug days of Firefox. They're for more than inspecting the DOM or debugging JavaScript. Chrome DevTools are a boon to the productivity of front-end developers.

It is absolutely worth taking some time to really learn the ins and outs of DevTools. I'll talk about some things in there that might be particularly helpful for building PWAs.

The first big item has to do with simulating offline behavior. I've already talked a lot about offline capabilities being a big part of PWAs, and you can test those capabilities by opening DevTools, navigating to the *Network* tab, and clicking the checkbox that says *Offline*, as you can see in Figure 2-4. In doing so, the particular site you have open will behave as though you have no Internet connection. Very handy!

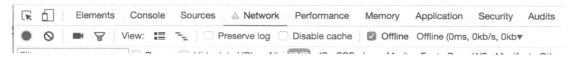

Figure 2-4. *Offline mode in Chrome DevTools*

Another handy feature is right next door to offline mode: *Throttling*. This setting will make the site you have open behave as though your Internet connection is limited to whichever option you choose, most of which are visible in Figure 2-5. One of the core tenets of PWAs is that your app loads reasonably fast (under 10 seconds) on 3G. This is a good way to test that scenario.

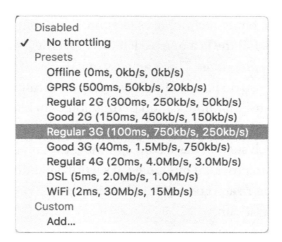

Figure 2-5. *Throttling settings to test slow connections*

Underneath the *Application* tab of DevTools, you'll find an option at the top left for viewing your app's manifest file. Take a look at Figure 2-6. Here you can see the app's name, short name, the start URL, the theme color, background color, app orientation, favicons, and more. I'll look at the app manifest in more detail in Chapter 6, but now you already know how to view it!

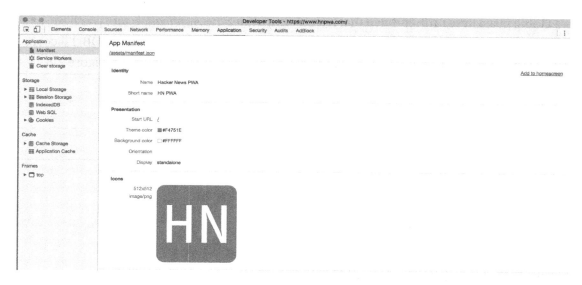

Figure 2-6. *App Manifest section of DevTools*

Immediately below the Manifest option underneath the *Application* tab, you'll see a section called Service Workers where you can see all the service workers installed for the current app. As in Figure 2-7, you're presented with the status and information of the service worker and presented with options such as unregistering the service worker, options to fire a sync event to test the background sync API, and updating the service worker. From here you can even send a test push notification. I'll get into why you might use these options in the next chapter on service workers.

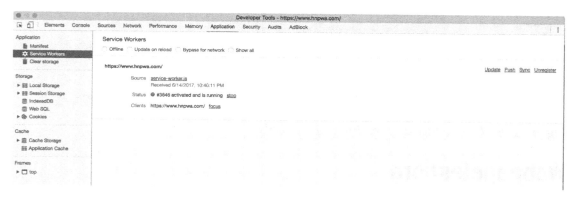

Figure 2-7. *Service Worker section of DevTools*

Going just a little further down that left column under the *Application* tab, you'll see a section for IndexedDB where you can see the key value pairs stored in IndexedDB. I'll cover this in more depth in Chapter 5, but you can see what the section looks like in Figure 2-8.

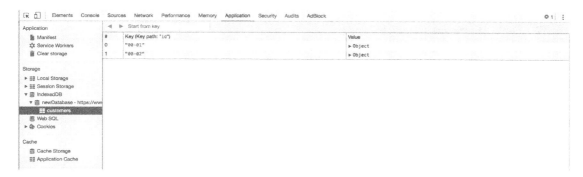

Figure 2-8. *IndexedDB section of DevTools*

The last piece of Chrome's DevTools we'll look at is the Cache section, which is also under the *Application* tab. If you expand the *Cache Storage* item, as in Figure 2-9, you'll see the service worker cache for the app, which will display all the items currently in the cache on the right. From there, you can delete or refresh items in the cache.

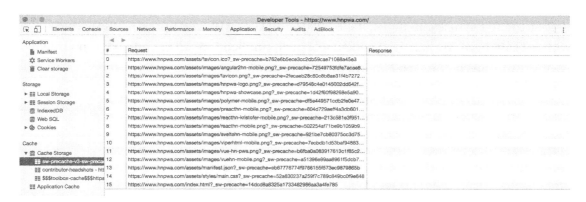

Figure 2-9. *Cache Storage section of DevTools*

Webpagetest.org

The last tool to cover is an oldie but a goodie. Webpagetest.org is an open source tool maintained by Google and is a much more performance-focused tool than an all-around PWA-focused tool. But a very large part of PWAs has to do with performance. So it's still a very valuable tool to have on your belt.

Because Webpagetest is open source, you can actually install a local, private version of Webpagetest or navigate to the site and run tests that way. For details on how to do so, check out the documentation because it's a great resource for making sure you're able to use the tool to best meet your development needs. For your purposes, you'll stick to the website.

Navigate to the page, and input any site you want in there. Because I already picked on Reddit for the Lighthouse example, I'll use mobile Twitter here for comparison's sake.

There are a lot of options you can play with here, and the app provides solid documentation if you have any questions. For your purposes, stick with the Chrome browser and the rest of the default options. After you click *Start Test*, it will run for a while before you see some results, as in Figure 2-10.

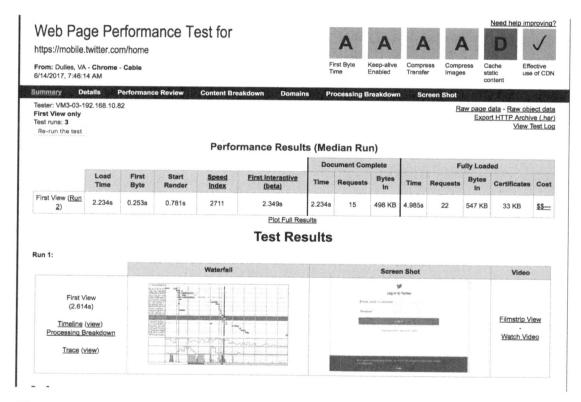

Figure 2-10. *Webpagetest.org*

Here you'll have information about page loads, screen shots, charts, and stats to show how your page is rendering. In the top right corner of the results page are optimization grades for the app, including time to first byte, if the app is using compression for data transfers and images, if static content is being cached, and a few other things.

If you click on the grades, you'll get quite a few more details about each of those sections.

There is a wealth of information on Webpagetest.org. It will be well worth your time to play around in there, read the documentation, and use the tool on your PWAs.

Looking Ahead

You've gotten a nice overview of PWAs and the tools you can use to measure them. Now it's time to start implementing some of these features. You'll start with the backbone of PWAs: service workers. Let's get to coding!

PART II

PWA Features

CHAPTER 3

Service Workers

How's your cell phone signal right now? Are you on a capped data plan? Is your WiFi spotty? Maybe your roommate is torrenting movies and taking all the bandwidth. Perhaps you're commuting on a train, and your cell provider's coverage map claims the whole route is blanketed in LTE, but all you see is a perpetually spinning circle of no Internet and you start to question what you're even paying for. But take deep breaths. Whatever the reason for your lack of a great Internet connection, there's no reason to be ashamed. It's not your fault.

There are a number of capabilities that service workers bring to the Web, but the biggest one is offline functionality. There have been attempts in the past to make the Web more offline-friendly, but they've had various issues that service workers attempt to solve.

Note You may have heard of or are even familiar with using AppCache. And if so, you deserve a sticker. The many drawbacks of AppCache are legion and well documented, so I won't kick a technology while it's down. Just know that all of that is over, and service workers are here for you.

A service worker is a script that runs in the background of your web application. It doesn't need the DOM and in fact doesn't even have access to the DOM. Service workers run in a separate thread from the UI, so they don't block or freeze the UI while they process. The whole point of a service worker is that it acts as an intermediary between your app and the Internet. It then performs whatever function you've set it up to perform, and finally communicates some result back to your app by passing messages. You can see this service worker architecture in Figure 3-1.

© Dennis Sheppard 2017
D. Sheppard, *Beginning Progressive Web App Development*, https://doi.org/10.1007/978-1-4842-3090-9_3

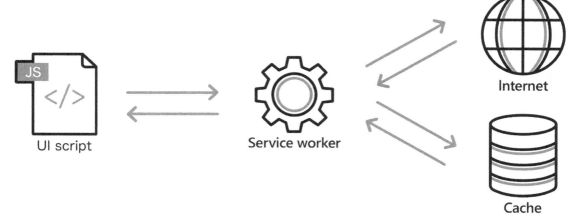

Figure 3-1. *Service worker architecture*

If intercepting network requests and then potentially passing back something different sounds nefarious, you're right. This basically sounds just like a man-in-the-middle attack. For that reason, service workers require a secure connection to function. All traffic for the app must run over HTTPS to prevent such nefarious activities.

In the next chapter, I'll cover the non-nefarious things we can accomplish with service workers, such as

- Caching assets like images, scripts, or styles

- Caching entire pages

- Syncing an app that was offline once its Internet connection comes back to life

- Push notifications

There are a number of other potential benefits to using service workers that I won't get into in this book because the specifications for them aren't quite ready, or they're just potential ideas that fit well into the service worker architecture. But some of them are really exciting, such as periodic sync, processing gyroscope data, and performing certain actions based on a date and time.

I'll also talk about the life cycle of service workers:

- Registration and downloading

- Installation

- Waiting (sometimes)

- Activation

- Updating

You're probably super excited, and rightfully so! But there are a couple of things to cover before we dive in. Service workers make heavy use of *promises*. If you're already familiar with promises, feel free to skip that section. But they're so vital to the use of service workers, so I'll spend a little time covering the basics of how to use them. There are ample resources online to go deep into the inner workings of promises if your curiosity is piqued.

I also need to briefly cover the Fetch API for making API requests. This won't take long, though. As soon as you learn the prerequisites, you'll be creating service workers in no time.

For all the examples in the book, try following along in your own dev environment. Explore, play with the values, try to enhance the examples, and break the examples. For a lot of the code we'll be using, you can use a `jsfiddle` from `jsfiddle.net` or a `plnkr` from `plnkr.co`.

Let's get started!

Promises

JavaScript is single threaded. So when your app makes an API request, it's going to move on to the next line of code, not waiting for that request to finish. But you need some kind of mechanism to process the result of that API request. In the past, you'd use callback functions to accomplish this. But they can be pretty clunky and hard to read when they end up being nested several times, leading to *callback hell*.

Promises fix this problem by telling the asynchronous method that it "promises" to call a given function as soon as the async one is finished. In Figure 3-2, `function1` could make an API call and then go right on to call `function2`, even though `function3` appears next sequentially. Once the asynchronous function is finished, *then* `function3` will execute.

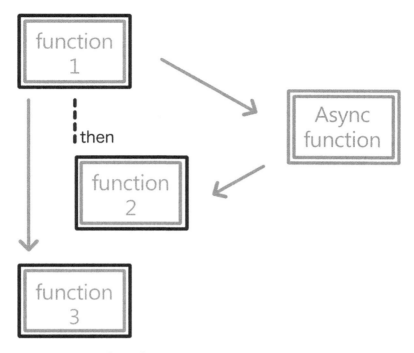

Figure 3-2. *Execution order when using promises*

It does so in a very readable and self-explanatory syntax. Let's take a look (https://jsfiddle.net/fyx8oufs/2/):

```
function myAsyncFn() {
  const everythingWentWell = true;
  return new Promise(function(resolve, reject) {
    // do something in here
    // usually an ajax call
    // or other async function
    if (everythingWentWell) {
        resolve('Success!');
    } else {
        reject('Things did not go well :( ')
    }
  });
}
```

```
function init() {
  myAsyncFn().then(function(response) {
    alert(response);
  })
  .catch(function(err){
       alert(err);
  });
}

init();
```

Here are two functions. One is named myAsyncFn and it creates a promise to make an asynchronous call and returns the result. A promise can either be *resolved* or *rejected*. In this case, you set a Boolean called everythingWentWell to true and resolve the function inside the promise. The entire promise object is returned to the calling function.

So the init function calls myAsyncFn and then calls an anonymous function that alerts the response that's passed into it. That response is the string you put in the *resolve* that was inside the myAsyncFn.

Note   A function that returns a promise is sometimes referred to as a **thenable** function.

If you change the everythingWentWell Boolean to false, you can see the promise get *rejected*. In that case, the init function will call myAsyncFn and the then call gets skipped. Instead, you catch the rejection error.

While there may be occasions where you'll need to create promises, most of the time the code you'll be writing will be consuming promises, which is what the init function in this example is doing.

There are times when you may need to *chain* promises. Maybe an asynchronous call has to wait for another one to finish before it can run. In that case, you can simply call then again (https://jsfiddle.net/fyx8oufs/3/):

```
function myAsyncFn() {
  const everythingWentWell = false;
  return new Promise(function(resolve, reject) {
  // do something in here
```

```
  // usually an ajax call
  // or other async function
  if (everythingWentWell) {
    resolve('Success!');
  } else {
    reject('Things did not go well :( ')
  }
  });
}

function secondAsyncFn() {
  return Promise.resolve('This second function is much more concise');
}

function init() {
  myAsyncFn()
  .then(secondAsyncFn)
  .then(function(response) {
    alert(response);
  })
  .catch(function(err){
    alert(err);
  });
}

init();
```

Here you add a secondAsyncFn that is called in the first then inside of init. That secondAsyncFn also returns a resolved promise (but notice the shorthand: you didn't have to new up a promise just to resolve it; you can just call the resolve method on a static promise object). Once the secondAsyncFn returns, you can call then on that as well.

For the purposes of learning service workers, this is all you really need to know about promises. Next, you'll take a quick look at the Fetch API.

Fetch

You may be familiar with making AJAX requests from jQuery, other frameworks and libraries, or even the old school XMLHttpRequest object from the web development days of yore. Fetch is a native web platform API that allows you to make network requests that return promises. Let's take a look (https://jsfiddle.net/fef98bg6/1/):

```
(() => {
  fetch('https://opentdb.com/api.php?amount=1')
  .then((response) => {
    return response.json();
  })
  .then((data) => {
    alert(data.results[0].question);
    alert(data.results[0].correct_answer);
  })
  .catch((err) => {
        alert(err);
  });
})();
```

This is a bit different from the last example, but it's still using promises. You don't need a separate function for the async call because that's essentially all you're doing. You also don't need to create a promise this time; the fetch call does that.

Along with those changes, I snuck in some new syntax, too. You're not going to call init anymore. You're just using an IIFE.

Note   An IIFE is an *immediately invoked function expression*. It's just a function that calls itself. Notice the open and close parenthesis at the end.

Finally, you've dropped the function keyword in place of arrow functions.

29

> **Note**   Arrow functions are available in all modern browsers. If you're not familiar with them, they're essentially just a shorthand notation for a function. Any time you see the arrow, think of the word "function" and move the parenthesis to the other side of it.

The first thing you do in this example is make a `fetch` call. You can substitute in your own API endpoint, but this example borrows one from the Open Trivia Database. Because `fetch` returns a promise, the next line after making the fetch call, you have a then. Fetch sends the promise results into the `then` function, via the `response` object. The response from a fetch comes back as a `ReadableStream` type. Before you're able to use it, you need to call `json()` on the response.

> **Note**   There are other functions you can call on `ReadableStreams`, depending on whether you're expecting text (`response.text()`), a blob (`response.blob()`), or something else. In this case, you expect a JSON response.

The `json` method returns a promise of its own. So you return that promise and *chain* then functions, just like you did before. The `json` method parses the `ReadableStream` as JSON, which could be an object, a string, a number, or anything else JSON could represent. In this case, there's a results array. At this point, you can do anything you want with those results; this example is a very rudimentary trivia game thanks to the Fetch API, promises, and the Open Trivia Database.

There are a few nuances to `fetch` that I can cover as we run into them. For now, if you play around with the example above, you should have plenty of fetch knowledge in order to finally move on to your first service worker!

Service Workers

There are three main parts of the service worker lifecycle. To kick things off, you just need to register the service worker. If that goes well, the service worker is installed and finally activated. You can see a visual of this process in Figure 3-3. There are cases where this path takes a few detours when you update the service worker, but follow along and you won't get lost.

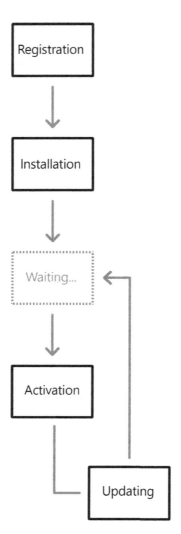

Figure 3-3. *Service worker lifecycle*

Register the Service Worker

The first thing you do to create your first service worker is register it. This will download your service worker script. You can put this code anywhere, but I want the service worker in this example to run on page load. So you create a JavaScript file that runs on page load and put your registration code in an IIFE inside of a file called `script.js`:

Note   You can find the files for this example in the `chapter3-example-1-register-and-activate` branch of `github.com/dennissheppard/pwa`.

```
(() => {
  if ('serviceWorker' in navigator) {
    window.addEventListener('load', () => {
    navigator.serviceWorker.register('service-worker.js').
    then((registration) => {
        console.log('registered');
console.log(registration);
    },(err) => {
        console.log(err);
      });
    });
  } else {
    alert('No service worker support in this browser');
  }
})();
```

Then in a script called `service-worker.js`, you listen for the install and activate events, the other two parts of the lifecycle:

```
self.addEventListener('install', (event) => {
    console.log('service worker installed', event);
});

self.addEventListener('activate', (event) => {
  console.log('service worker activated', event);
});
```

Finally, you just need to reference your script in an `index.html` file:

```
<html>
  <head>
    <link rel="stylesheet" href="style.css">
    <script src="script.js"></script>
```

```
  </head>
  <body>
    <h1>Hello PWAs!</h1>
  </body>
</html>
```

Let's start by breaking down the original `script.js` file and working through it.

Because servicer worker support isn't universal, you want to check first if the navigator object has a property called `serviceWorker`. If not, that browser doesn't support service workers. If it does, you're in business!

Next, you need to listen for the `load` event on the `window` object to know when to register the service worker. If you wanted to register it based off some other event, you certainly could do so.

The next line is where the actual service worker registration happens. Call `navigator.serviceworker.register` and pass in the path to the service worker file. Call it `service-worker.js` and pass that path as a string into the `register` function. The `register` method returns a promise, so you can call `then` on it.

The function in the `then` method receives a `registration` object from `register`. Log that out and take a look in a moment.

If anything goes wrong with script registration, log out that error.

Moving on to the service worker itself, it's pretty concise. The worker executes code by listening to events. The first two events you're concerned with are the `install` event and the `activate` event. For now you'll just log out those events.

That's all the code you need to set up your first service worker!

Note   If you pulled down the repo from github.com/dennissheppard/pwa, switch to the `chapter3-example-1-register-and-activate` branch and run `npm install` in the root directory to install the http-server module. After installation is complete, you can run the example by typing `http-server` in the terminal from the root of the project. This will start a server on port 8080, so that you can navigate to `http://localhost:8080`. If you typed the code manually or copied and pasted into your own project, you'll need some type of webserver to run the code.

Run that code and let's take a look at Chrome DevTools. Go to the *Application* tab. On the left, you should see an option that says *Service Workers*. Click that, and you'll see all of your service worker information. Also, make sure your console is open at the bottom. Your DevTools should look something like Figure 3-4.

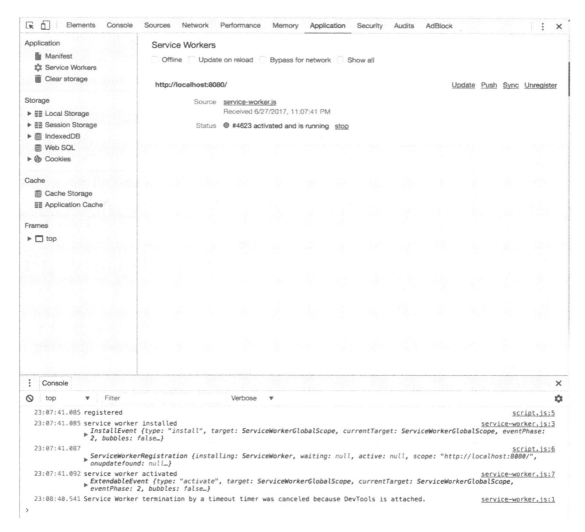

Figure 3-4. *Service Workers section of DevTools. Notice what's logged in the console at the bottom.*

Looking at the console, the first thing you want to see is the `registration` object in your `script.js` file. There are some pretty interesting things in there that you'll be playing with later. The first thing you see is a property of type `ServiceWorker` called `active`. If you expand it, you can see that it has a few of its own properties, notably `state`. Your service worker's state right now is "activated." You're doing great so far!

Further examination of this object shows that there are objects of type `PushManager` and `SyncManager`. Those are probably not completely useless, but you'll find out later.

The last important thing here is *scope*. The scope of your service worker is how much of the application it is allowed to control. Scope is impacted by where you place your service worker. If it's placed and referenced at the root of your application, it has access to your entire application. If you put the service worker in a subdirectory, say `scripts/trivia`, then the service worker only has the scope to control everything in the `trivia` directory. More specifically, this means that the service worker is installed and will receive network events for every page that loads within the `trivia` directory. You may specify a scope as a second parameter of the `register` function, but it must be a subdirectory of where your service worker lives. Figure 3-5 shows the different scopes allowed depending on where you place your service worker.

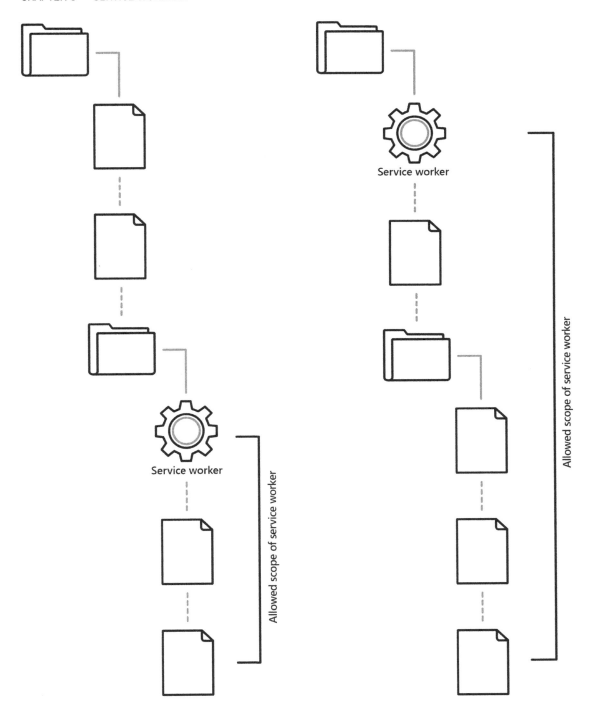

Figure 3-5. *Service worker scope*

In the `chapter3-example-2-sw-scope` branch, for example, your service worker can't live in the `/scripts/trivia` directory while also having a scope of the whole `/scripts` directory:

```
(() => {
  if ('serviceWorker' in navigator) {
    window.addEventListener('load', () => {
    navigator.serviceWorker.register('scripts/trivia/service-worker.js',
{scope: 'scripts'}).then((registration) => {
      console.log(registration);
    }, function(err) {
        console.log(err);
      });
    });
  } else {
    alert('No service worker support in this browser');
  }
})();
```

Notice the `scope` object as the second parameter of the `register` method. If you run this example, you'll get an error that looks something like this: *The path of the provided scope ('/scripts') is not under the max scope allowed ('/scripts/trivia/'). Adjust the scope, move the Service Worker script, or use the Service-Worker-Allowed HTTP header to allow the scope.*

The last option of that error is saying that you can add a header to the service worker script's response to allow the service worker to be used anywhere. For your purposes, you're going to just make sure your service worker isn't trying to take over more scope than it's allowed to.

If you wanted to, you could put the service worker in the `/scripts` directory but set the scope to cover just the `/scripts/trivia` directory. That's a valid scope. You're not actually using that directory, though, so to fix the scoping error, let's just move the service worker back to the root directory, and completely remove the `scope` object.

Once you run this again, take another look at Chrome DevTools. You should see your "service worker installed" and "service worker activated" events in the console, like in Figure 3-6.

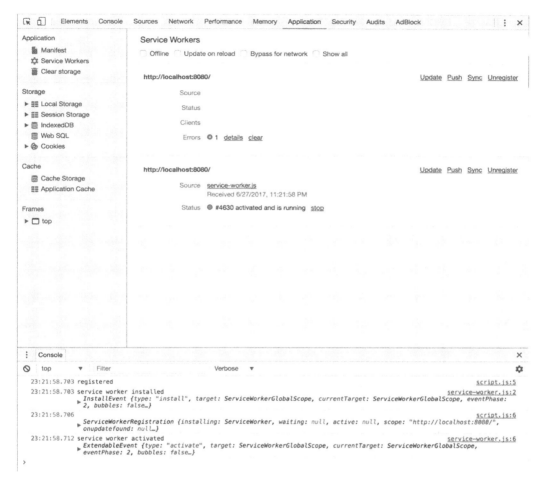

Figure 3-6. *Service worker with updated scope*

If you run the example with the bad scope, at the top of the DevTools page you'll see a service worker with the scope error I mentioned. Below that is your activated and running service worker with the correct scope.

Updating the Service Worker

Now, let's make a little tweak to the service worker script so you can see how to update the service worker. Let's just change the first of the console statements. This change is reflected in the `chapter3-example-3-updated-sw` branch.

```
console.log('updated service worker installed', event);
```

Just a simple change so that the browser sees an updated service worker. Save it and refresh your browser. If you look in DevTools, you'll see the same service worker. The console shows that it was registered again, but there's no install or activate events logging anything. What's up with that?

The changes to the service worker script file in this instance won't be visible for up to 24 hours, or until all of the clients controlled by that service worker have been terminated.

But we're devs and know ninja tricks that regular users don't. So click the Update link over on the right. Once you press that, you should see a second service worker that's labeled as "waiting to activate." As in Figure 3-7, in the console you'll see the "updated service worker installed" log statement, but no activated log statement.

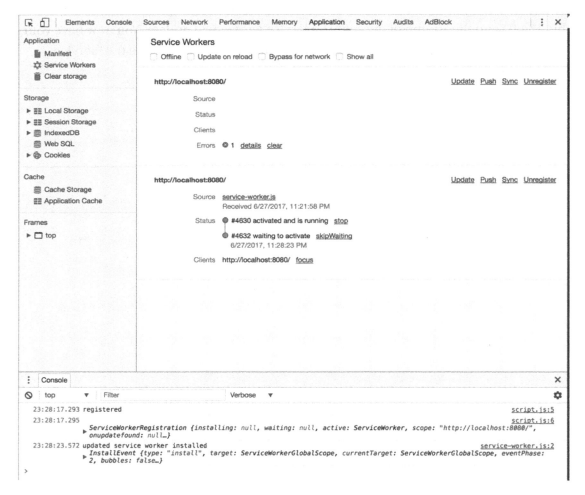

Figure 3-7. *A "waiting" service worker. Notice there's no "activated" log statement.*

Because the label says it's "waiting," it makes sense you don't have the activated log statement. But why is it in this "waiting" state? The browser does this so that only one version of your service worker is running at a given time. The new service worker is registered and installed, but it wants to wait until the original service worker is booted out.

Note   As I've talked about, service workers deal a lot with data, be it caching or syncing or pushing. You can imagine some of the issues that can pop up if you have two different service workers in two different tabs trying to manage that data in different ways.

Again with the ninja tricks, you can click the "skip waiting" option. When you do this, the ID and timestamp of the running service worker will update. You now have your latest service worker running, and looking down at the console, you see the "service worker activated" log statement in Figure 3-8.

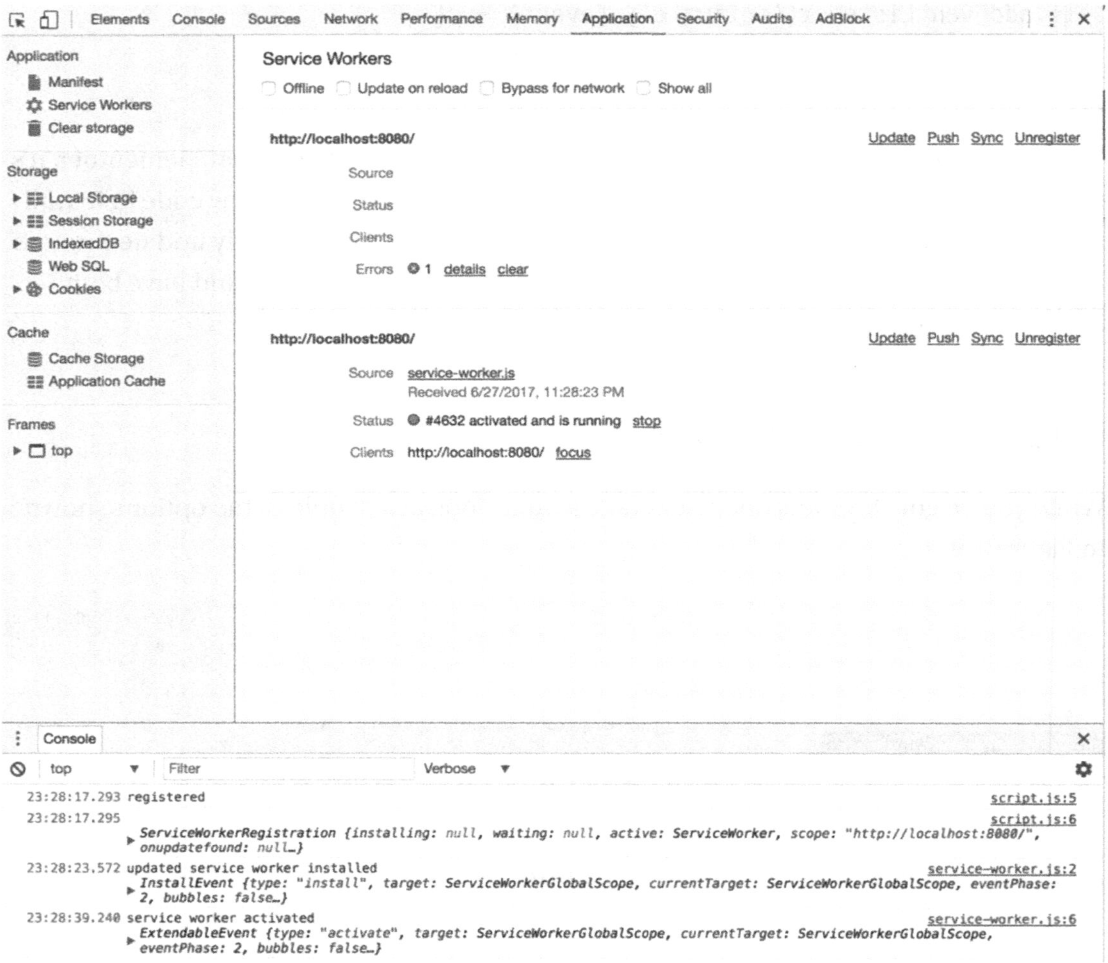

Figure 3-8. *Service worker updated and activated*

If you want to bypass the safety check of making sure your app only has one service worker controlling a page a time, you can force the update in code as well, with the skipWaiting() method. This immediately removes the existing service worker and activates the new one, skipping the normal waiting state:

```
self.addEventListener('install', (event) => {
  self.skipWaiting();
  console.log('updated service worker installed', event);
});
```

```
self.addEventListener('activate', (event) => {
  console.log('updated service worker activated', event);
});
```

If you make that update and refresh, nothing new appears to happen. Remember, it's still holding onto your previous service worker that didn't have your new code in it until you close all the open tabs of your app and reload, or until you manually update through DevTools. So let's click Update again. This time, the service worker should have both installed and activated, since you skipped the waiting state.

Other DevTools Options

While you've got DevTools open, let's take a quick look at a couple of the options shown in Figure 3-9.

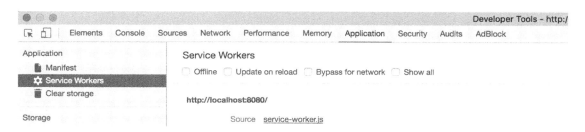

Figure 3-9. *Service Workers DevTools options*

The *Offline* option makes the app act as though you have no Internet connection. You'll be using this a lot in the next chapter.

After that is the *Update on reload* option. This forces your service worker to update when you make changes to it in code. This keeps you from having to click that Update link every time you make a change to your service worker. With this option checked, each page of your app you go to refetches the service worker script, and the `install` and `activate` events fire. So no more needing to reload the page twice or manually skip waiting or anything.

You'll likely want this option checked for development.

Next is an option labeled *Bypass for network*. This basically turns off your service worker so none of your CSS or JavaScript is cached during development.

Finally, the *Show all* option will show you every service worker installed in your browser for various sites you've visited. If you're a PWA or service worker nerd, it's pretty interesting to see which sites and apps are using service workers.

Browser Compatibility

I've laid the groundwork to really get into the amazing things service workers are capable of. Until mid-2017, service workers were limited by browser compatibility. Service workers are best supported by Chrome and Firefox, followed closely by Opera. But Edge is enabling service worker support by default as of version 16, and the last major remaining holdout, Safari, has undertaken development for service worker support. We love you, Safari! There's a site dedicated to the browser support of service workers at `https://jakearchibald.github.io/isserviceworkerready/`.

Service Worker Recap

This chapter covered a lot, so let's take a minute to recap. Service workers

- Are scripts that live between your app and the network

- Only work on HTTPS

- Are the PWA mechanism for caching, background syncing, push notifications, and more

- Install using `register`

- Listen for `install` and `activate` events

- Enter a *waiting* state on updates to ensure there is only one running at a time

Looking Ahead

Next, you're going to apply all of this knowledge to create some service workers that do a lot more than just log things out to the console. You'll look at caching your resources to speed up your page loads and reduce bandwidth usage. I'll also walk through how to make an app work with no Internet connection at all. Sound good? Let's go!

CHAPTER 4

Caching and Offline Functionality with Service Workers

Now that you know what service workers are and how to implement a very basic one, in this chapter you're going to go beyond the basics. We want apps to be fast, reliable, and work offline whenever possible. So now I'm going to talk about the Cache API that lets us return items we specify from the cache instead of making the whole journey to the server.

The fetch Event

Before you can cache anything, you need to be able to intercept network requests. That's trivial using your service worker. Every network call originating from the domain in which the service worker has scope will fire the fetch event:

```
self.addEventListener('fetch', (event) => {
  event.respondWith(fetch(event.request));
});
```

So you just need to listen for it in the service worker. Here, you catch the event and simply respond with whatever would have come back anyway. In Figure 4-1, you can see the service worker catching the fetch event, making its own call to the API. Once that data is returned to the service worker, you can pass that back to the calling script, manipulate it somehow, or do nothing at all.

© Dennis Sheppard 2017
D. Sheppard, *Beginning Progressive Web App Development*, https://doi.org/10.1007/978-1-4842-3090-9_4

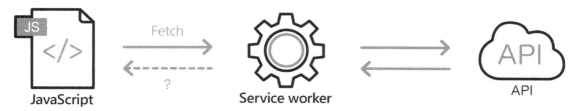

Figure 4-1. *The fetch event listener intercepts the API request*

If you pull down the `chapter4-example-1_fetch_event` branch from `github.com/dennissheppard/pwa` and run `npm install` and `http-server`, then the site will be accessible on `http://localhost:8080`. Once you go there, you'll see a pretty great site dedicated to pirates, as shown in Figure 4-2 (no need to judge how it looks; this isn't a book about CSS!).

Figure 4-2. *The site returns normally if you just intercept fetch and respond with the same fetch*

As far as the service worker goes, this isn't very helpful or practical because you're just using it as a pass through. It's like you aren't doing anything. But think of the implications. What if we were pirates who wanted to hijack a site and had the ability to slip a rogue service worker onto someone's site? Arrgh!

```
self.addEventListener('fetch', (event) => {
  event.respondWith(new Response('arrrgh!'));
});
```

If you throw that code in your service worker and run it (remembering to either click *Update* in the Service Worker section of DevTools or check *Update on reload*), Figure 4-3 shows what you would have.

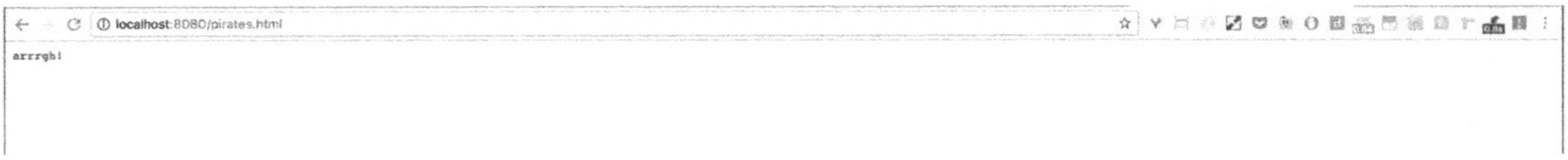

Figure 4-3. *Pirates have taken over your site!*

You're able to do this by creating a new `Response` object and responding with that text. Then any fetch event just responds with that. So instead of any HTML pages or images or anything, you simply have "arrrgh!" Which is pretty fun!

You could also respond with a fully-fledged HTML file announcing that your site is under maintenance or really whatever you want.

So you've started off by listening for the `fetch` event, and you know you can intercept network requests and return anything you want. But you didn't come here to be a pirate; you came here to see what the cache can do for you.

The Cache API

Caching is going to be your new best friend. Using it, you can make your app significantly faster, and you can even make the app usable with no Internet connection at all, because you can just respond with items you've previously saved. Let's start with a quick example that saves items to the cache. Let's add the following code to `service-worker.js`:

```
self.addEventListener('install', (event) => {
  if (!('caches' in self)) return;
  event.waitUntil(
```

```
    caches.open('version1').then((cache) => {
      return cache.addAll(
        [
          '/pirates.html',
          '/styles/pirates.css',
          '/styles/pirates.tff',
          '/images/i-love-pirates.jpg'
        ]
      );
    })
  );
});
```

Go ahead and clear out the fetch event; you'll bring it back in a moment. Now you have your install event back. You can add items to the cache on the install event.

Note   The 'caches' property is actually also available on 'window'. That means you can technically cache items from anywhere in your app. Try some of these examples in other parts of your app, perhaps based off of user interactions that would make sense to cache items. Maybe you can even give your user the option to save certain resources for offline use.

First, check browser compatibility for caching. Add in the check for the caches object on self to make sure the current browser supports it, and if not, let's just get out of here.

Assuming you're using a fully supported modern browser, add in this new method: event.waitUntil. This method takes a *promise*, which extends the lifetime of install until the promise resolves. This is useful because you don't want the event to complete until you've cached your files. Plus, if the caching fails for some reason, the promise is rejected and the service worker isn't installed.

Next you have the caches object. To create a new cache, call open and give it a name. Note that open returns a promise, so you can call then on it and then add an array of files by using the addAll method on the cache object returned from the promise.

If you have a sample project with an HTML file, a CSS file, and maybe an image, add those files to an array in a service worker like above. Or, pull down the `chapter4-example-1_caching` branch from `github.com/dennissheppard/pwa`.

You now have a pretty amazing site dedicated to pirates. Let's open DevTools and load the site. You can see what the *Network* tab tells you in Figure 4-4.

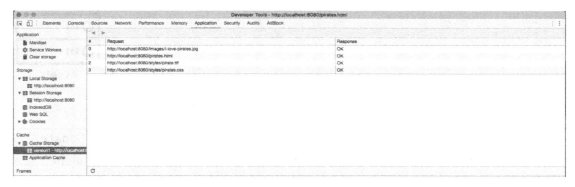

Figure 4-4. *Network requests after creating the cache*

All of your files are being fetched like you'd normally expect. You've created the cache of your files, but you haven't told the service worker to use the cache yet. You can see what you've cached by going to the *Application* tab in DevTools and expanding the *Cache Storage* item on the left. You may have to right-click on it and tell DevTools to refresh the cache before it will show up. Now you should see your *version1* cache with the items you told your service worker to cache, as in Figure 4-5.

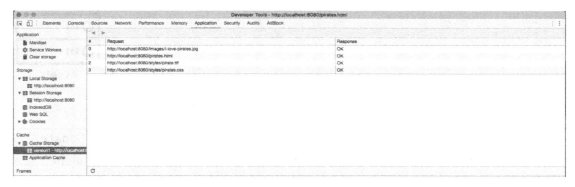

Figure 4-5. *The newly created version1 cache*

So now you have the triumphant return of your `fetch` event. Using that, let's go ahead and tell the service worker to use the cache you've created:

```
self.addEventListener('fetch', (event) => {
  event.respondWith(
    caches.match(event.request)
  );
});
```

Now you're listening for the `fetch` event once again, which will intercept any network request the service worker has control over. You `respondWith` items in your cache that *match* the same URL as the network request. In your case, that should be four out of five files. Figure 4-6 shows this happening.

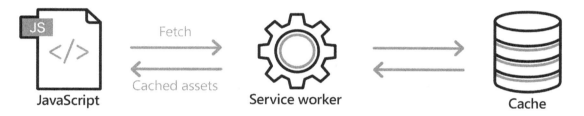

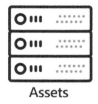

Figure 4-6.   Retrieving cached items

So now you should add that snippet to your service worker. Make sure the `Update on reload` option is checked in the Service Worker section of the *Application* tab in DevTools.

Now if you look at your *Network* tab, like in Figure 4-7, you can see that the items you told the service worker to cache are being fetched "from ServiceWorker" in the *Size* column.

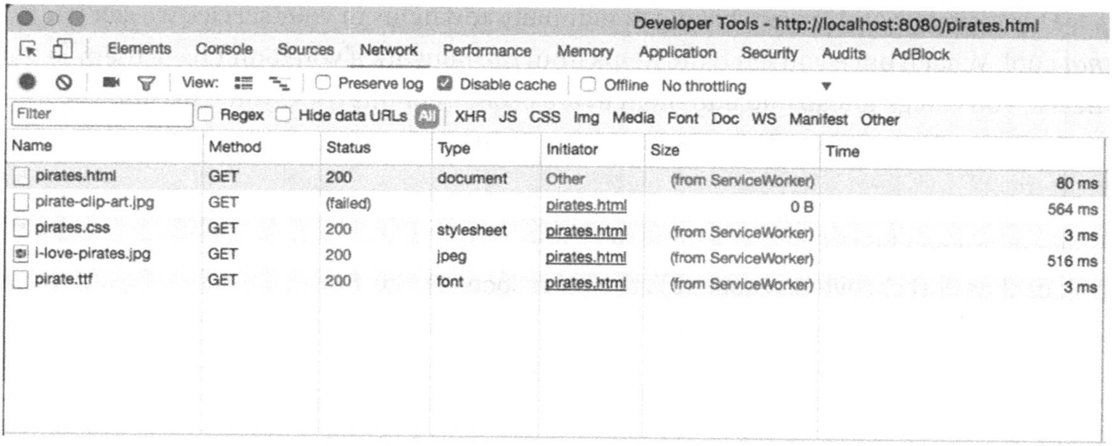

Figure 4-7. *Items returned from cache*

You'll notice that one lovely image is failing to return. That's because you haven't cached that file and you have no backup. You told the service worker to intercept those requests and return what's in the cache. If a particular request isn't in the cache, that match fails. So if there's a file you don't want to cache, or you might have files you haven't cached before, you need to tell the service worker to go ahead and fetch that file using the network instead of the cache. Luckily, the match method on the caches object returns a promise with the response. And you're actually kind of decent at handling promises by now.

```
self.addEventListener('fetch', (event) => {
  event.respondWith(
    caches.match(event.request).then((response) => {
      return response || fetch(event.request);
    })
  );
});
```

Wait for the promise to return from the match method, then call a function that gets the response. If that file wasn't found in the cache, response is *undefined*, so go ahead and call the fetch method to make the request from the network.

If you add that to your service worker and refresh, now all the items in the *Network* tab should be returning from ServiceWorker.

This is pretty solid, except having to manually add items to your service worker isn't *that* cool. What if once you fetch the items from the network if you didn't have them in the list, you can go ahead and add them to the cache? For this trick, you'll use the put method, which takes the request and the response objects:

```
self.addEventListener('fetch', (event) => {
  event.respondWith(
    caches.match(event.request).then((response) => {
      return response || fetch(event.request).then((response) => {
        console.log('fetched from network this time!');
        return caches.open('version1').then((cache) => {
          cache.put(event.request, response.clone());
          return response;
        });
      });
    })
  );
});
```

As you've seen before, fetch returns a promise. You call then on fetch passing in the response from the network. In that function, you can open up the version1 cache again, and this time you'll put the request and its corresponding response in the cache. You have to call clone on the response because the original response isn't kept in memory. Once it's read once, it's gone. But you still need to return the original response, as well as save it in the cache. So to do so, you just call clone on it. Figure 4-8 may help you visualize that process.

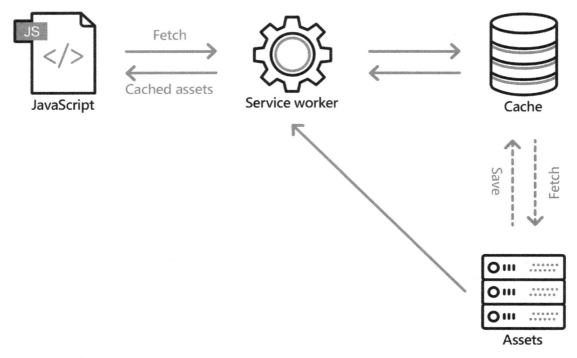

Figure 4-8. *Retrieve items from cache, or fetch if they're not in the cache, and then save in the cache for next time*

If you run this code, you again should see everything returning from the ServiceWorker in the *Network* tab. Look at the console, and you can see that an item was fetched from the network, because you slipped that console.log line in the then on the fetch call.

Refresh the page one more time, and that line is gone from the console. Switching over to the *Application* tab and looking at the *Cache Storage* section, you have a new item added in! Your cache is doing work!

Going Offline

You now have everything you need to make your app offline capable. This is just a small sample app, but as long as you cache what is necessary for your app to function, what we've covered here will scale well for all your fetching needs.

It can, however, be helpful to let the user know that there's currently no connection, in case something isn't in the cache and appears broken. Figure 4-9 illustrates the workflow of checking for a connection, and returning cached resources if so or returning an offline page if not.

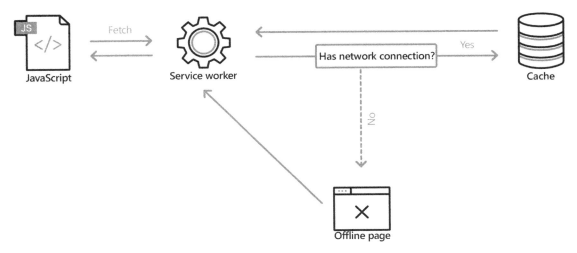

Figure 4-9. *Service worker checks for network connection, and if there's no connection, returns an offline page or message*

This example shows a special offline landing page that does just that:

```
self.addEventListener('install', (event) => {
  event.waitUntil(
    caches.open('version1').then((cache) => {
      return cache.addAll(
        [
          'index.html',
          '/pirates.html',
          '/styles/pirates.css',
          '/styles/pirate.ttf',
          '/images/i-love-pirates.jpg',
          'offline.html'
        ]);
    })
  );
});

self.addEventListener('fetch', (event) => {
  if(!navigator.onLine && event.request.url.indexOf('index.html') !== -1) {
    event.respondWith(showOfflineLanding(event));
```

```
  }
  else {
    event.respondWith(pullFromCache(event));
  }

});

function showOfflineLanding(event) {
  return caches.match(new Request('offline.html'));
}

function pullFromCache(event) {
  return caches.match(event.request).then((response) => {
    return response || fetch(event.request).then((response) => {
      return caches.open('version1').then((cache) => {
        cache.put(event.request, response.clone());
        return response;
      });
    });
  });
}
```

Here are two functions that are called from within the `fetch` event listener. The first one is called if the browser has no Internet connection. You can check for this using `navigator.onLine`.

Note   `navigator.onLine` isn't 100% accurate in its ability to know if there's a network connection. There are some browsers that don't implement it correctly, and some where it will return `true` as long as there's an internal network connection, but no Internet connection. So in production apps, you may not want to solely rely on this method of determining the user's Internet connection state. Here, it's just an example to show how you might respond with an offline page.

If you're offline and the request is for index.html, you know you want to display your special offline landing page. So you respond to the fetch event by looking in the cache for a request that would match offline.html. If you look up at the install event, you'll see that this is a file that you added to the cache. So your offline.html page will be returned in place of your traditional index.html. Thus, if you run this code once, turn off your WiFi, and refresh, you should be presented with something like Figure 4-10.

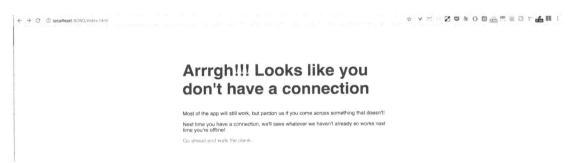

Figure 4-10. *Your special offline landing page, only seen when there's no Internet connection*

If you aren't looking specifically for index.html, just call the pullFromCache function that does the same thing you've already covered: looks in the cache for each request, and calls fetch if it can't find it. Additionally, if there's a connection, that resource is automatically added to the cache.

You now not only have an app that can load resources without a network connection, but can also show different screens and load different resources without a network connection.

Different Caching Strategies

I've covered the most common and helpful caching scenario you're likely to need: using the cache first, and using the network as a backup.

There are other combinations of caching and fetching you can use in your applications, though.

Note   Most of these examples you'll find in the `chapter4` branches of `www.github.com/dennissheppard/pwa/branches`, but if it helps you to type them in manually, by all means do that!

For instance I've also covered two others, *network-only*, in which case the service worker is just a pass through, and *cache-only*, where you look for files in the cache and anything not there simply fails.

Those aren't the most helpful caching options, because *network-only* behaves as though the service worker isn't even there, and *cache-only* loads just the resources that are in the cache. That means anything not in there you can't fetch from the network. So some resources will be missing, and it's possible that the items that are available in the cache could be quite old.

One improvement to this strategy is called *stale-while-revalidate*. This tells the service worker to request both the cache and network, return the cached version to the caller, and save the network response in the cache to use for next time. This allows the cache to be updated while still delivering the fast, cached content to the user. Let's take a look at how you could implement something like this:

```
self.addEventListener('fetch', (event) => {
  const version = 'version1';

  event.respondWith(
    caches.open(version).then((cache) => {
      return cache.match(event.request).then((response) => {
        let fetchPromise = fetch(event.request).then((networkResponse) => {
          cache.put(event.request, networkResponse.clone());
          return networkResponse;
        });
        event.waitUntil(fetchPromise);
        return response;
      })
    })
  );
});
```

With this code, you're looking for your cached resource and returning it. But before you return it, you also fetch the same request and use cache.put to save the networkResponse in the cache.

You could also ask for both the cached resource as well as the network resource, and whichever one is faster is the one that gets to respond to the request. This sounds great in theory, because if you have a slow Internet connection you can just use the cache. But if you already have items in the cache, it can be a waste of bandwidth to ask for the network to return your resources. Just ask the cache to start with. Only in very few circumstances would the network be faster than the cache, mainly with super old hard drives. But if you're curious about how that could work, take a look at Figure 4-11.

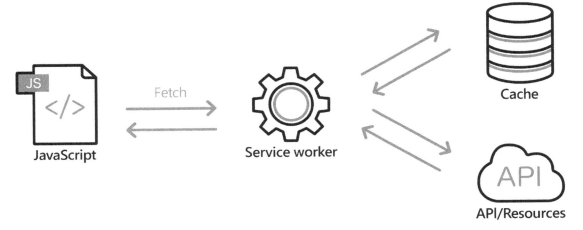

Figure 4-11. *"Fastest" caching strategy: both the cache and API (or resources/assets) are fetched. The fastest one back to the service worker wins and is used.*

Let's take a look at the code you need to do this:

```
function setupPromises(promises) {
  return new Promise((resolve, reject) => {
    promises.forEach(promise => promise.then(resolve));
  });
};

self.addEventListener('fetch', function(event) {
  event.respondWith(setupPromises([
      caches.match(event.request),
```

```
      fetch(event.request)
  ]));
});
```

Here you create a function that takes an array of promises. That function returns a new promise that resolves as soon as the promise passed in resolves. So basically you pass in both the `cache` and `fetch` calls, and both are used in the `respondWith` function.

If you run this and open your DevTools *Network* tab as in Figure 4-12, you'll see that each asset is actually requested twice: once from the service worker and once from the network.

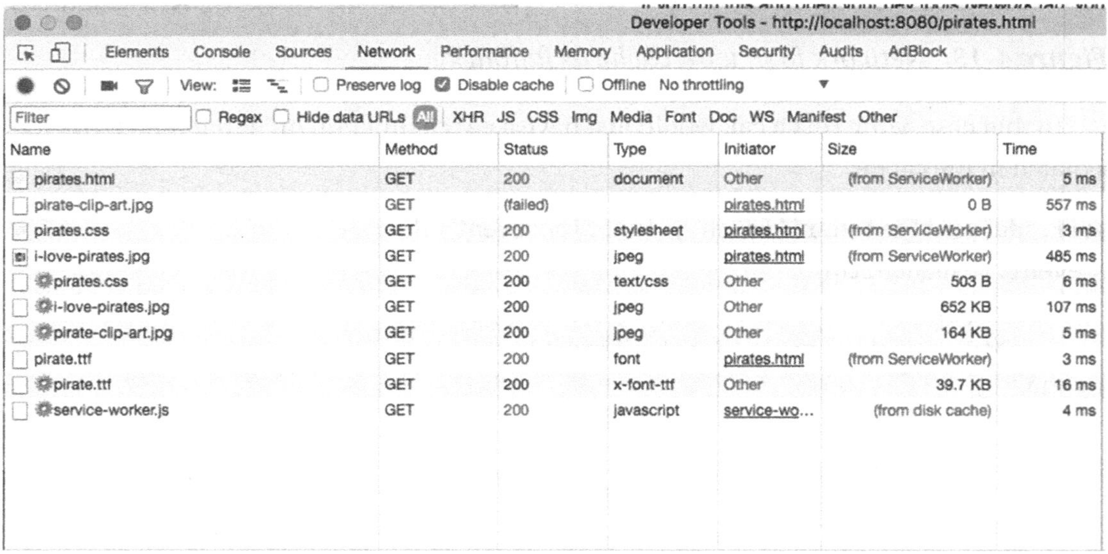

Figure 4-12. *Each asset is requested twice*

As you can imagine, there are additional patterns you can use with caching. Maybe you'd like to try the network first and fall back to the cache if that call fails, as in Figure 4-13.

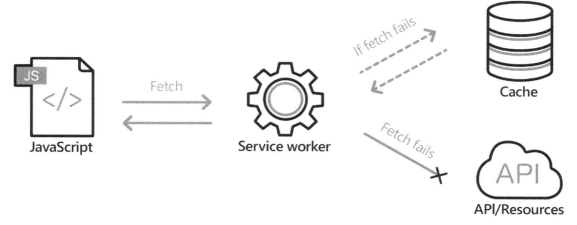

Figure 4-13. *Network first, with cache as fallback*

In that case, your fetch call would just have a catch function on it that then looks for a match in the cache:

```
self.addEventListener('fetch', function(event) {
  event.respondWith(
    fetch(event.request).catch(function() {
      return caches.match(event.request);
    })
  );
});
```

You could also display nice error messages for offline scenarios. Perhaps there's a request for something that isn't in the cache while the user has no network connection. In that scenario, you can configure your service worker to return a placeholder image, or even a message explaining that the user is offline right now, but next time they have a connection, that resource will be available:

```
self.addEventListener('fetch', (event) => {
    const version = 'version1';
    const placeholderAssetURL = 'placeholder';
    event.respondWith(
      fetch(event.request).catch((e) => { // fetch fails
```

```
    return caches.open(version).then((cache) => {
      return cache.match(placeholderAssetURL);
    });
  })
  );
});
```

Whatever option you go with for caching will depend upon the needs of your application. You should spend some time experimenting and coming up with other potential solutions using caching and fetching resources to ensure your user has the most pleasant experience possible.

Of course, just because you have items returning from the cache doesn't mean everything is great. Oftentimes a user's cache can contain old files that your app doesn't use anymore. It's your job to tell the service worker to clean those up.

Updating the Cache

Since you're going to be caching lots of things while also updating your app regularly, some of the stuff in the cache can become stale. Maybe you updated that old pirate image with a sweet new one, and you don't want that being displayed to the users anymore.

Where might be a good place to clean up an old cache? That's right, the `activate` event! If you remember, the `activate` event fires once there are no more old service workers controlling your app. That sounds like a great time to clear out an old cache. Figure 4-14 shows the theory, and then you'll look at the implementation.

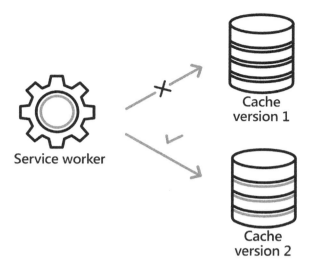

Figure 4-14. *Updating the cache by deleting the old one (version1) and creating the new one (version2)*

```
self.addEventListener('activate', (event) => {
  const CURRENT_CACHE = 'version2';
  event.waitUntil(
    caches.keys().then((cacheKeys) => {
      return Promise.all(
        cacheKeys.map((cacheKey) => {
          if (cacheKey !== CURRENT_CACHE) {
            console.log('Deleting cache: ' + cacheKey);
            return caches.delete(cacheKey);
          }
        })
      )
    })
  );
});
```

You need to label your current cache so that it doesn't get wiped out when the service worker is activated. That wouldn't do you much good.

Then you get all of the different cache keys and delete any of them that have a different name than CURRENT_CACHE.

If you run this code, make sure you update any call to `caches.open` with whatever you're naming your CURRENT_CACHE, or you're going to keep recreating the cache you're trying to delete. Once you update that, add in the snippet above and run it. You should see something similar to Figure 4-15 in the *Application* tab in DevTools.

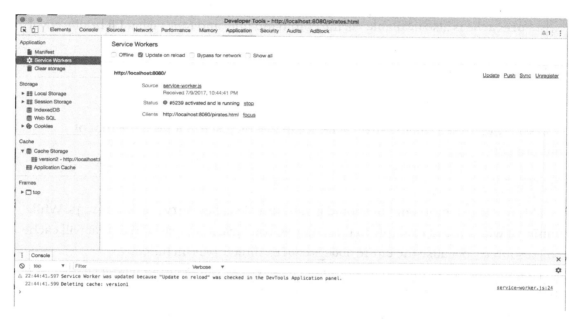

Figure 4-15. *You made the version1 cache walk the plank, and version2 now lives!*

You may need to right-click on *Cache Storage* on the left pane in DevTools and choose *Refresh Caches* before you can see your *version2*.

Now you have a brand new cache!

But if you're thinking, "This looks easy if you have a dumb static site about pirates. What about a real-world application with dozens of files?" you wouldn't be wrong. Manually configuring service workers and caching as your project grows can be complex. And that's when two tools from Google can really help you out: **sw-precache** and **sw-toolbox**.

sw-precache

I haven't covered build processes, as that's out of the scope of this book. But if you are familiar with and use Gulp or Grunt, or any other JavaScript build process (like Webpack), `sw-precache` can be a game changer. It is a node module that you integrate

into your build process that will generate a service worker for you and set up caching for certain resources that you specify. Because this is handled at build time, these are likely to be the more static assets of your app, like your `index.html`, images that are on most or all pages, global stylesheets, etc. (basically your app shell, which I'll cover in more depth later on). It will handle versioning and caching strategies for you as well.

`sw-precache` is also available via the command line, and that's what I'll briefly cover here.

Go ahead and install `sw-precache` like this:

```
npm install --global sw-precache
```

If you want to see what `sw-precache` is capable of, just run it from the root of your project:

```
sw-precache
```

This will take a moment but should generate a file called `service-worker.js`. While running it with the last example in this chapter, you have a service worker that will cache 1587 resources, because the entire `node_modules` directory is included.

That's not super helpful, but without a build system, and without telling `sw-precache` what you want included, this result is expected.

Instead, let's create a config file that tells `sw-precache` exactly what you want and call it `sw-precache-config.js`, placing it at the root of your project:

```
module.exports = {
  staticFileGlobs: [
    'styles/**.css',
    'styles/**.ttf',
    'images/**.*',
    '**.html'
  ],
  skipWaiting: true,
  cacheId: 'version2'
};
```

Here you're giving `sw-precache` a list of all the static resources you want cached. You can also tell it to include a call to `skipWaiting`, and give your cache an ID. There are numerous other options you could use, with a full list available at the `sw-precache`

documentation: `https://github.com/GoogleChrome/sw-precache#options-parameter`.

Now you can run `sw-precache` again, specifying your config file:

```
sw-precache --config=sw-precache-config.js
```

If you look at what this generates, it's a much more reasonable file, caching seven resources. Of course, in larger apps, that number will be greater, but using patterns in your file list should make this fairly easy.

If you look at the generated file, you'll see a lot of code. But in there is the familiar `install`, `activate`, and `fetch` events. There's a lot of additional code to handle path matching and other options that you could put into your config.

Again, `sw-precache` is geared more toward your static files, but even in larger apps you'll likely want to point the config to files in a `dist` folder, or some equivalent, assuming you have some kind of build process.

sw-toolbox

I talked about some of the caching strategies you can use with the Cache API and we looked at code to handle a few. But if you don't want to worry about manually writing code to take those on, `sw-toolbox` will provide helpers to do it for you. While `sw-precache` is more useful for your app shell, `sw-toolbox` is better for handling your dynamic content.

Note   If "dynamic content" seems a little too vague, just think about that as data returned from an API that can vary based on parameters or user interactions. For example, in the trivia game example, the questions you fetch from that API are dynamic content.

Let's install `sw-toolbox` first, just like you did `sw-precache`:

```
npm install --save sw-toolbox
```

This will give you a `companion.js` and a `sw-toolbox.js` file in the node_modules/sw-toolbox directory. You can either use that path, or move those files to the root of your app. To make things easier for you, go ahead and move them.

Now you can register your service worker like you have before, or you can use a shortcut. Since you already know how to register the service worker the other way, let's use the shortcut this time.

In your `index.html`, you just need to include a reference to the companion file and point to your service worker:

```
<script src="companion.js" data-service-worker="service-worker.js"></script>
```

Note   The benefit of using this shorthand method is purely brevity. If you need to add in additional logic around installing service workers, this probably isn't the way you want to implement yours.

Next, you'll need to reference that `sw-toolbox.js` file you moved. For that, just add it to the `service-worker.js` file with `importScripts`:

```
importScripts('sw-toolbox.js');
```

After those are in place, you're set up to use `sw-toolbox`. This will work much like the `fetch` events you're used to, except in the place of a `fetch`, `sw-toolbox` will intercept *routes* and perform caching, based on an option that you specify. Those options are the ones I discussed a few pages back.

Let's take a look at an example that implements the "fastest" caching strategy for all of your image files (calling both the cache and the network and using whichever comes back the fastest):

```
importScripts('sw-toolbox.js');

self.addEventListener('install', (event) => {
});

toolbox.router.get('/images/*', toolbox.fastest, {
  cache: {
    name: 'sw-toolbox-version1',
```

```
    maxEntries: 20,
    maxAgeSeconds: 60 * 30
  }
});
```

You've imported sw-toolbox.js, and you don't need anything in your install event right now.

To tell sw-toolbox you want images cached in a certain way, you use "Express" style routing, using a URL pattern with a syntax similar to Express.js.

Note   You can also route using regular expressions if you're more familiar with them.

Passing in your images URL to the toolbox.router.get is the first step. Then you specify which strategy you want to use, *fastest* in this case. Next, you have options for your cache: name, maxEntries (how many entries will be cached before the oldest one is deleted), and maxAgeSeconds (which will cause the cache to expire at the specified time; yours is set at 30 minutes).

Of course, you can use different routes and different caching strategies if you'd like. You'll also say you want everything in your styles directory to use cacheFirst and to expire those after a week:

```
toolbox.router.get('/styles/*', toolbox.cacheFirst, {
  cache: {
    name: 'sw-toolbox-version1',
    maxEntries: 20,
    maxAgeSeconds: 60 * 60 * 24 * 7
  }
});
```

Go ahead and run this and see what you get. Close any previously opened tabs, open up DevTools, and navigate to the home page and then to a content page.

In the *Application* tab, go to the *Cache Storage* section on the left. You may need to right-click and choose *Refresh Caches* to see the latest stuff in there, as shown in Figure 4-16.

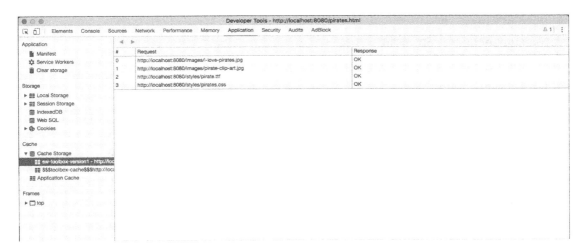

Figure 4-16. *Hey, that's your stuff! Those are your images and files in the styles directory.*

In a bonus surprise, Figure 4-17 shows that if you go up to the *IndexedDB* section on the left (again, you might need to right-click and choose *Refresh IndexedDB*), you'll see how `sw-toolbox` is managing those cache expiration times.

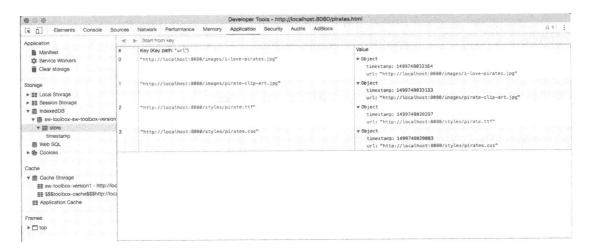

Figure 4-17. *That's your stuff, too! This time with expirations on it. And in a different place!*

Dynamic Page Caching

All of your static content is cached and working great. But what if you added a page that displays items dynamically, based on an API call? Just caching the HTML file isn't going to do you much good.

Let's go ahead and create this page and see what you can do. If you're able, pull down the `chapter4-example-6_sw-toolbox` branch from `github.com/dennissheppard/pwa`. In there, you'll see a new file called `pirate_books.html`. The actual HTML portion of this file consists of just a couple of lines:

```
<body>
    <h1>Books About Pirates</h1>
    <ul id="pirateList">
    </ul>
</body>
```

Because your list of books is going to be generated dynamically based on results of an API call, you're not going to get away with just caching `pirate_books.html`. You'll also need to cache that API call.

Take a look at the `<script>` section of that same file, and you can see what API call you're using and how you generate the list items:

```
<script>
    let pirateBooks = [];
    let bookSearchUrl = 'http://openlibrary.org/search.
    json?q=pirate+history';
    fetch(bookSearchUrl).then((response) => response.json()).then((data)
=> {
        pirateBooks = data.docs;
        generatePirateBookList();
    });

    function generatePirateBookList() {
      let pirateList = document.getElementById('pirateList');
      for (let i = 0, book; book = pirateBooks[i]; ++i) {
        let pirateItem = document.createElement('li')
```

```
        pirateItem.innerHTML = book.title + (book.author_name ? " by " +
        book.author_name[0] : '');
        pirateList.appendChild(pirateItem);
      }
    }
  </script>
```

The book list data comes from openlibrary.org, and you can make that call with just a few lines like in the script block above. It's a simple fetch call, where you assign the results to an array. Then just loop over the array, generating list items with the book title and author. Finally, append each item to your pre-existing ul.

You need to cache the response from that fetch call so you can still use the page while offline. So let's go ahead and add a couple of new routes to your service worker:

```
toolbox.router.get('*.html', toolbox.cacheFirst, {
  cache: {
    name: 'sw-toolbox-version1',
    maxEntries: 20,
    maxAgeSeconds: 60 * 60 * 24 * 7
  }
});

toolbox.router.get('/*', toolbox.networkFirst, {
  origin: 'openlibrary.org',
  cache: {
    name: 'sw-toolbox-version1',
    maxEntries: 20,
    maxAgeSeconds: 60 * 60 * 12
  }
});
```

That first route is to cache your HTML files, which you just haven't done to this point. The second one is the important one for your dynamic data. You tell sw-toolbox to look at all content from the *origin* (openlibrary.org) since the call originates from a different domain than your app. Notice also that you're telling sw-toolbox to use the *networkFirst* strategy. This is because API data should typically be fresher than your static content. This is also why if you look at your cache expiration for this route, you're specifying that

you should expire this cache in 12 hours. Of course, that value will vary based on your needs, but typically dynamic data should stay relatively fresh.

So now you have a dynamic page, you're caching the page, and the response that holds the data to generate the content on that page.

Close all of your open clients in the browser, open a new browser tab and its DevTools, and navigate to the main page. Navigate to both pages to let the content make its way to the cache.

Now in DevTools, choose the *Offline* option in the *Service Workers* section of the *Application* tab.

Navigate around the app, and you should see everything operating perfectly normally. In case you're skeptical about the functionality of that *Offline* option in DevTools, try navigating to google.com or somewhere else on the Web to insure you have no Internet connection for that browser tab. You could also just turn off your WiFi.

Head on back to arrrrguably the best pirate site on the Web, because it's fully offline capable!

Whew, that was a lot of material, but who even needs an Internet connection now?

Looking Ahead

I've covered how to save things for offline use (or to just make everything speedier by going to the cache instead of the Web) when you need to fetch them, but what about when you need to update data on the server? That's what *background sync* does: holds on to your requests while you don't have a stable network connection and then sends them off into the great big Internet once you do. Let's take a look at that next!

Background Sync for Offline Apps with Service Workers

Most of the Pirate app is fully offline-capable. There's one glaring weakness remaining, though, as far as functionality without a connection goes. If you need to make an API call while you don't have a connection, there's no mechanism in place to do that. This Pirate app is so great, we'd love for people to be able to leave comments about it. Or even have pirate-based conversations! But what if you happen to like posting Internet comments when you're out at sea where your Internet connection is choppy? That's where the Background Sync API is going to help!

The Background Sync API

Background Sync will hold onto your API call until there's a stable Internet connection. Even better, as the "background" part of the name implies, the app will make the API call even if your app isn't active and running. Service workers are so cool.

Registering for sync

The way you're gonna make this happen is by registering for a `sync` event, and then listening for it, just like you do with `install`, `activate`, and `fetch`. You're an old hand at this by now, so the setup for this is going to be a breeze. To start, you'll allow users to post a message on your site: either "Ahoy!" or "Arrgh!" You need to post that message to your

© Dennis Sheppard 2017
D. Sheppard, *Beginning Progressive Web App Development*, https://doi.org/10.1007/978-1-4842-3090-9_5

API so you can fetch it later. And because you want to allow that to work while offline too, you'll go through a sync event.

```
function postComment(comment) {
    navigator.serviceWorker.ready.then((sw) => {
      return sw.sync.register(comment);
    });
  }
```

This is how you register for the sync. When a user is ready to post a comment, you check if the serviceWorker object is ready. If so, you get a reference to the service worker passed into the function in your then method. You call sync.register on that object and pass in a string key. This is the key you'll look for in your service worker. In your case, you pass in the string representation of whichever button the user pressed.

Listening for sync

In the service worker, the string key you registered for will be referred to as a *tag*. Let's take a look at that code:

```
importScripts('sw-toolbox.js', 'pirate-manager.js');

self.addEventListener('sync', (event) => {
  const data = pirateManager.setupCommentData(event.tag);
  event.waitUntil(pirateManager.postComment(data));
});
```

In the service worker, you listen for the sync event. This event holds a tag property that will let you know which button was pressed, because that's what you registered earlier on the button press in script.js. You take that tag and post it as the comment by sending it to the pirateManager.postComment method. Of course, just like before, you want the event to wait for you to finish your work before completing.

You've put the implementation of the postComment method inside of an object called pirateManager because you may want to be able to post comments outside of the service worker, too (remember, service workers are *progressive enhancements*; you still want your app to work even when service workers don't). So that you don't duplicate code, you have a few helper functions in the pirateManager. You'll look at that file in

a bit. For now, it's important to know that the postComment method returns a promise. When that promise resolves, the sync is finished. If the promise is rejected, another sync event may fire later on.

Implementation Details of Using sync

Let's take a look at the implementation of postComment as well as the whole pirateManager object, saved in a file called pirate-manager.js.

Note   All of the code in this chapter can also be found on the book's GitHub site at github.com/dennissheppard/pwa in the branches starting with chapter5.

The pirateManager object will take care of fetching your comments as well as posting them:

```
var pirateManager = (() => {
    return {
        getComments: getComments,
        postComment: postComment,
        setupCommentData: setupCommentData
    };

    function getComments() {
        return fetch('https://pirates-b74f7.firebaseio.com/commentList.json')
            .then((response) => response.json())
            .then((data) => {
                this.commentList = data;
                return this.commentList;
            });
    }

    function postComment(commentData) {
        let data = JSON.stringify(commentData);
```

```
        return fetch("https://pirates-b74f7.firebaseio.com/commentList.
        json",
            {
                method: "POST",
                body: data
            })
            .then((response) => {
                response.json();
            });
    }

    function setupCommentData(comment) {
        const d = new Date();
        const date = (d.getMonth() + 1) + "/" + d.getDate() + "/" +
d.getFullYear() + " " + d.getHours() + ":" + d.getMinutes() + ":" +
d.getSeconds();

        const data = {
            commentText: comment,
            date: date
        };
        return data;
    }

})();
```

There are three relatively straightforward methods here. The only details you need to know for background syncing are that the `postComment` method returns a promise via the `fetch` method, and that you're taking in the comment from the service worker to POST it to the API.

Note   This file is using the *revealing module* pattern. Notice at the top of the file there is a return statement that contains an object with properties referencing every function that other parts of the app might need. These functions are accessible through those properties.

You can see the high-level architecture for how you're going to use this *manager* file and how it fits into the rest of the app in Figure 5-1.

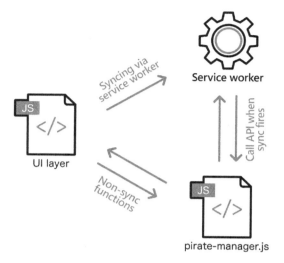

Figure 5-1. *App architecture using sync with a "manager" or service layer file*

Now in the `script.js` code, you tie everything together:

```
(() => {
    document.addEventListener('DOMContentLoaded', init, false);

    function init() {
        registerServiceWorker();
        addListeners();
        getComments().then((commentList) => renderComments(commentList));
    }

    function registerServiceWorker() {
        if ('serviceWorker' in navigator) {
            window.addEventListener('load', () => {
                navigator.serviceWorker.register('service-worker.js').
                then((registration) => {
                    console.log(registration);
                }, function (err) {
```

```
                    console.log(err);
                });
            });
        } else {
            console.log('No service worker support in this browser');
        }
    }


    function getComments() {
        return pirateManager.getComments()
            .then((commentList) => commentList);
    }


    function postComment(comment) {
        const data = setupCommentData(comment);
        if (navigator.serviceWorker) {
            navigator.serviceWorker.ready.then((sw) => {
                return sw.sync.register(comment)
                    .then((args) => {
                        appendComment(document.getElementById('comments'),
                        data);
                    })
                    .catch((err) => {
                        console.log(err);
                    });
            });
        } else {
            pirateManager.postComment(data).then(() =>
            appendComment(document.getElementById('comments'), data));
        }
    }


    function addListeners() {
        document.getElementById('arrghBtn').addEventListener('click', () =>
        postComment('Arrrgh!'));
```

```
    document.getElementById('ahoyBtn').addEventListener('click', () =>
    postComment('Ahoy!'));
}


function resetElements() {
    let comments = document.getElementById('comments');
    comments.innerHTML = "";
}


function renderComments(commentList) {
    resetElements();
    let comments = document.getElementById('comments');
    Object.keys(commentList).forEach((key) => {
        let comment = commentList[key];
        appendComment(comments, comment);

    });
}


function appendComment(commentsEl, comment) {
    let commentElement = document.createElement('p');
    commentElement.innerHTML = comment.commentText + " - " + comment.
    date;
    commentsEl.appendChild(commentElement);
    let hrElement = document.createElement('hr');
    commentsEl.appendChild(hrElement);
}

})();
```

Again, nothing too complex here, and I already covered the code that registers the sync event. One thing to note is that you're still registering the service worker like you always have before. This code registers the button click handlers, fetches comments that

have already been posted, and renders the comments on the page. The last thing to do to run this is to make some minor markup changes from the examples in the last chapter:

```
<h1>Comments</h1>
<div id="comments">
</div>
<div style="display: flex; flex-direction: row">
  <button id="arrghBtn">Say Arrrgh!</button>
  <button id="ahoyBtn">Say Ahoy!</button>
</div>
```

This is where you place posted comments and your two buttons for posting the user's message of choice. Once you have all this, run the code and post a couple of messages. These will fire the sync event and post to the Firebase API (you may even see other readers' previous messages from their own pirate ships across the sea, so say *Ahoy!* to them!).

Testing for Offline Sync

To test the background sync functionality, turn your Internet connection off. Don't worry, it's just temporary. The *Offline* mode of the browser isn't quite sufficient for this test.

Once your connection is off, post another message. You'll see that it shows up right away. That's because in your script.js code, you're manually appending the comment to your list of comments as soon as you register for the sync event. But nothing was posted to the API. Put a breakpoint in DevTools on the sync listener in the service worker, and maybe another in the pirateManager.postComment method. If you turn your Internet connection back on, your breakpoint should be hit, and the actual comment will post to the API! You can see a high-level overview of this process here in Figure 5-2.

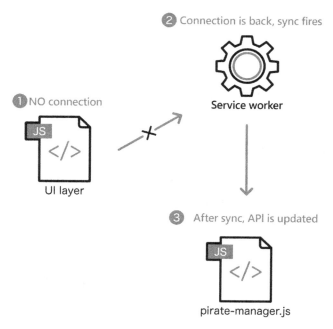

Figure 5-2. *No connection, so the script.js file is on its own. Then the connection returns and sync is fired. The service worker calls the pirate-manager.js file to update the API.*

Making Improvements

If you refresh the page on the messages you just synced while offline, you may have noticed that the timestamp of your message was different. That's one drawback to the implementation here. You update the UI as soon as the user clicks the button, regardless of whether the post was made. So in the offline scenario, the post doesn't actually make it to your API until the user is back online, which could be seconds or hours later.

A better user experience would be to let the user know that there is no connection and that their message will be posted as soon as connectivity returns. Once the message is actually posted, you can update the list of messages.

Also, wouldn't it be better if the user could post his or her own message instead of a precanned one? That's a little more difficult than you may think. If you're offline, you'd need to store that message somewhere so that the service worker still has access to it when the sync event fires when the user is back online. After all, the sync event will fire even if the app is no longer running in the foreground, which means the message wouldn't be in memory anymore.

You can make both of these improvements by using a data storage library.

Data Storage

For some front-end devs, databases can be a little intimidating. Most relational database work is unlike anything we do on the front end. But the storage solution you'll be using is not a relational database. You don't need to be a DBA, and you don't need to know SQL.

IndexedDB vs. localForage

IndexedDB is a large-scale, client-side storage solution. You can use it to store large amounts of data. But unlike relational databases, there aren't tables. Instead, you typically write to *object stores* that can hold numbers, strings, JavaScript objects, blobs, or files. You can use it to store, search, get, and update data, and even makes use of indexes for fast data retrieval. Additionally, IndexedDB uses *transactions* to ensure database integrity. A transaction is a wrapper around an operation that will fail if any part of the operation fails. This lets the database maintain its state before the transaction was attempted. See Figure 5-3 for a high-level look at IndexedDB.

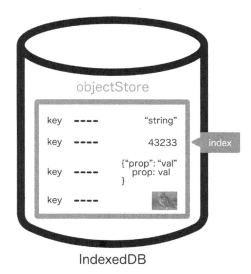

Figure 5-3. *IndexedDB structure*

If all of this sounds pretty great, let's take a quick look at a code example, but don't worry about too much about the details (you won't be using this code, and it likely doesn't actually work; this is for illustrative purposes only!):

```
(function() {
  // different browsers have prefixes
  window.indexedDB = window.indexedDB || window.webkitIndexedDB || window.
  mozIndexedDB || window.msIndexedDB;
  window.IDBKeyRange = window.IDBKeyRange || window.webkitIDBKeyRange ||
  window.msIDBKeyRange;

  if (!window.indexedDB) {
    window.alert("Your browser doesn't support IndexedDB");
  }

  // Open the DB
  var request = window.indexedDB.open("pirates", 1);

  request.onupgradeneeded = function(event) {
    var db = event.target.result;

    // Create object store for this database
    var store = db.createObjectStore("comments", { autoIncrement : true });
    store.createIndex('date', 'date', { unique: false });
  };

  function addComment(commentObj) {
    var tx = db.transaction('comments', 'readwrite');
    var store = tx.objectStore('comments');

    var req;
    try {
      req = store.add(commentObj);
    } catch (err) {
      throw err;
    }
```

```
    req.onsuccess = function (evt) {
      console.log("adding comment successful, arrrgh!");
    };
    req.onerror = function() {
      console.error("something went wrong", this.error);
    };
  }
})();
```

That's a lot of code just to create a database and write something to the store. IndexedDB can be complex. So you need a simpler way to use it, as well as having built-in fallback support. And that's where localForage comes in. Before I talk about localForage, let's look at a similar code sample that creates a database and writes a comment to it:

```
var store = localforage.createInstance({
  name: "pirate"
});
store.setItem('comment', {"comment": "ahoy!"}).then(() => {
  return localforage.getItem('comment');
}).then((value) => {
  console.log(value);
}).catch((err) => {
  console.log(err);
});
```

Well now, that's a lot less code. In fairness, this can only save one value at a time, while the prior example can save multiple. But hopefully you get the point. You are more than welcome to use old school IndexedDB if you would like, but from here on out, the pirate app (and any future examples that need some type of storage) will use localForage.

localForage is available via npm. So install it with

```
npm install --save-dev localforage
```

and make sure you add it to index.html like so:

```
<script src="node_modules/localforage/dist/localforage.min.js"></script>
```

If you run the pirate app again (make sure you clear out any cached files and old service workers), you can actually paste the localForage example code above into the DevTools console. If you do this, then go to the *Application* tab in DevTools and down to the *IndexedDB* section on the left, you can see the result of this operation (you may need to right-click on *IndexedDB* and choose *Refresh IndexedDB*), as in Figure 5-4.

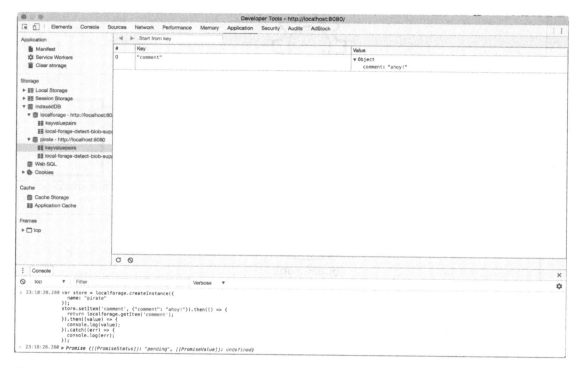

Figure 5-4. *The comment is saved in IndexedDB.*

So you're able to store items in IndexedDB with few lines of code. What is this spooky magic? localForage is a third-party library created by the Mozilla team. It essentially wraps IndexedDB (or WebSQL, though this is a deprecated technology) and automatically uses localStorage for a fallback. If you're familiar with localStorage, you may notice that the syntax of localForage in the setItem line of the example is very similar to localStorage.

Using localForage For Better Offline Support

Now we'll want to use this special magic to improve the pirate app's offline support and make the commenting feature a little more robust overall. Take a look at the overall architecture of the new plan that utilizes localForage in Figure 5-5.

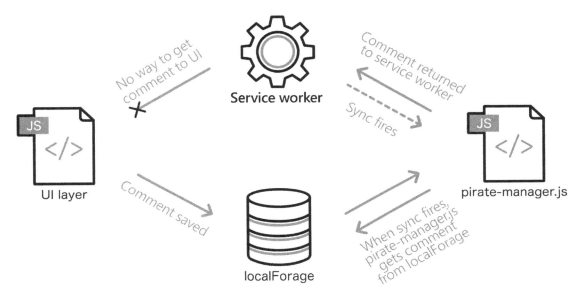

Figure 5-5. *Pirate app architecture using localForage. The UI saves the comment to localForage. When the sync event fires, the service worker calls pirate-manager. js, pirate-manager.js fetches the comment from the data store and once the API call is made, the service worker handles the promise, which has the data. From there, though, we currently have no way to update the UI from the service worker.*

The complete example using localForage is in the `chapter5-example-2_localforage` branch of the `www.github.com/dennissheppard/pwa` repo if you just want to follow along with all of the code pre-written.

If you want to type out the code, go ahead and add a `textarea` element to your HTML view, and change the two buttons to just one comment button:

```
<textarea id="comment-text" cols="40" rows="10"></textarea>
<div style="display: flex; flex-direction: row">
  <button id="commentBtn">Leave a comment</button>
</div>
```

That will allow your users to say hello in whatever way they choose. You're able to store that comment using localForage. Let's go ahead and do that as soon as the user presses the *Leave a comment* button and before you register your sync event in the main script.js file:

```
function postComment() {
        document.getElementById('commentBtn').innerHTML = "Posting...";
        localforage.setItem('comment', document.getElementById('comment-
        text').value)
            .then(() => submitPost());
    }
```

Here you're saving whatever the user entered into your offline store with the key comment. The setItem method will return a promise. You need to wait until you're sure the value is stored before you register for sync or make the API call. Then you can call submitPost, which will register your sync if the browser supports it, or just make the API call if not:

```
function submitPost() {
        if (navigator.serviceWorker) {
            navigator.serviceWorker.ready.then((sw) => {
                return sw.sync.register('post-comment')
                    .then((args) => {
                        offlineTimeout = setTimeout(() => {
                            localforage.getItem('comment').then((val) => {
                                document.getElementById('no-connection-
                                message').style.display = "block";
                                document.getElementById('commentBtn').
                                innerHTML = "Leave a comment";
                                document.getElementById('comment-text').
                                value = "";
                            });
                        }, 3000);
                    })
                    .catch((err) => {
                        console.log(err);
                    });
```

```
        });
    } else {
        pirateManager.postComment().then((data) => {
            document.getElementById('comment-text').value = "";
            document.getElementById('commentBtn').innerHTML = "Leave a
            comment";
            document.getElementById('no-connection-message').style.
            display = "none";
            appendComment(document.getElementById('comments'), data);
        });
    }
}
```

The submitPost function has kind of a lot going on, so I'll break it down. First, you're checking to see if you have service worker support. If not, you just make the call to the API and update the UI. If you do, things are much more interesting.

You register sync once you get an instance of the service worker. You changed the name of the sync key to post-comment. Now you don't need to register the sync based off what the user enters. Regardless of the message, you'll always sync with the post-comment key.

Once the sync is registered, set a timeout to give the API a few seconds to make its POST. If the POST isn't successful by that point, you assume the user is either offline or has a poor Internet connection. So, show an offline message and wait for the sync to fire again to retry the POST. If the POST is successful, you'll clear the timeout later. You're declaring that timeout at the very top of this file, but that declaration is not shown in the above snippet.

Over in pirate-manager.js, retrieve the comment text from your data store so that you can make the POST to the API. Because you saved the comment into storage as soon as the user clicks the button, this will work for both when you're on and offline:

```
function postComment() {
    return localforage.getItem('comment').then((val) => {
        let d = new Date();
        let data = {
            commentText: val,
```

```
        date: (d.getMonth() + 1) + "/" + d.getDate() + "/" +
d.getFullYear() + " " + d.getHours() + ":" + d.getMinutes() + ":" +
d.getSeconds()
        };

        return fetch("https://pirates-b74f7.firebaseio.com/commentList.
        json",
        {
            method: "POST",
            body: JSON.stringify(data)
        }).then(() => {
          localforage.removeItem('comment');
          return data;
        });
      });
    }
```

Notice that the getItem call to retrieve your comment from the data store returns a promise. Here you need it to get the value, package it up with a date stamp, stringify it, and send it off to your API. You also want to remove the comment from your local database because it's safe and sound in your remote database. No need to hold on to it. Also, go ahead and return that packaged-up data after the POST because you'll need it to update your UI.

At this point, the user can POST their own comment even if they're offline.

Since you're supporting a nice offline message for the offline user, let's just add that simple message to your view HTML above your textarea (and no judgement for that inline styling; it's purely to illustrate that you want to hide that message until you determine the user is offline):

```
<div id="no-connection-message" style="display: none;">
        <h2>Arrrgh! Looks like you have no connection. We'll try posting
your message again when you're back online!</h2>
</div>
```

You're just about finished! The app lets users post comments, whether or not they have a connection because you're using a web data store, and you can display a message to the user if they post when they're offline. The last thing you'd like to do is update the UI once the user regains a connection.

If you noticed the architecture diagram (Figure 5-5), though, you know that you don't have anything in place to do that. To this point, `pirate-manager` knows nothing of the DOM, and `script.js` knows nothing of the API. Nice, clean separation. You don't want to mess that up. So how do you let your UI file (`script.js`) know that the call is finished?

If you were using a library like RxJS or any other Pub/Sub type of library, this would be pretty straightforward. There is a similar way to accomplish this, though, with a built-in feature of service workers.

The message Service Worker Event

There are times you need the service worker and its clients to communicate back and forth. This is done via a `message` event that you can listen for in either the service worker, the client, or both. Let's take a look at the syntax before applying it to the app:

```
navigator.serviceWorker.controller.postMessage("Hey Mr. Service Worker,
whattya say?");
```

From `script.js`, you can send a message back to the service worker. On the service worker side, you just need to set up a listener to catch the message:

```
self.addEventListener('message', (event) => {
    console.log("This was received by the service worker: " + event.data);
    event.ports[0].postMessage("Hey Mr. Client, what do YOU say?");
});
```

You register for an event like you've done a hundred times before. The message is contained in the event argument passed in. You can even have the service worker respond by posting a message on the event's *port* that was opened when the client sent the message.

If you want to communicate in the reverse direction, the syntax is mostly the same. And that's what you need to do for the pirate app. In your case, the service worker is the one calling the POST method to save your comment, and your POST method returns a promise that you can handle in your service worker. So the service worker just needs to send a message to the client once the POST comment call is finished.

Once `pirate-manager` is finished POSTing, let the UI know to update

```
function notifyClient(msg){
    self.clients.matchAll({'includeUncontrolled': true}).then((clients) => {
```

```
    clients[0].postMessage(msg);
  });
}
```

Slip that function right into your service worker code at the bottom. It takes all of the service worker's connected clients and passes them into a promise. If there were multiple tabs open, all running the same service worker, you could selectively send messages to different clients. In your case, you only have one, and you can reference it directly and post a message to it using `clients[0].postMessage`. Way back up in your `sync` listener in the service worker, you can call this `notifyClient` function when your POST is finished:

```
self.addEventListener('sync', (event) => {
  if (event.tag == 'post-comment') {
    event.waitUntil(pirateManager.postComment().then((data) => {
      notifyClient(data);
    }));
  }
});
```

You can see that after you call `pirateManager.postComment()`, you have a promise that has a `data` object in the `then` function. That's the data returned from `postComment`. If you remember, that's your comment text and a date stamp packaged up for you. You send that to the `notifyClient` function, and that should send your data to the client. But you still have to listen for it over in `script.js`. However, that's straightforward:

```
function addListeners() {
        document.getElementById('commentBtn').addEventListener('click', ()
        => postComment());
        if (!navigator.serviceWorker) {
            return;
        }
        navigator.serviceWorker.addEventListener('message', (event) => {
            clearTimeout(offlineTimeout);
            document.getElementById('comment-text').value = "";
            document.getElementById('commentBtn').innerHTML = "Leave a
            comment";
```

```
        document.getElementById('no-connection-message').style.display
        = "none";
        appendComment(document.getElementById('comments'), event.data);
    });
}
```

Registering for the message event is as simple as calling addEventListener on the serviceWorker object. As soon as the client receives the message event, you should clear the timeout that checks to see if you should show the offline message. You've already received word that the POST is complete, so obviously you have a connection. If the offline message was displaying, you can go ahead and clear it because now you have data to show and you're back online. The last thing you need to do is append your new comment to your list of comments. You passed that data from the pirateManager, and you have access to it via event.data. This message pattern is a much cleaner way of allowing the service worker and the UI to communicate. Take a look at Figure 5-6 to see this updated architecture.

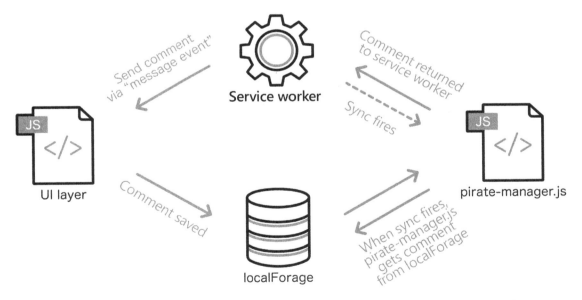

Figure 5-6. *Updated architecture using the message event to send the user's comment to the UI*

You should now be able to post comments while online. Try it out. Also, kill your network connection and try to post a comment. You'll get the offline message, with your comment safely tucked away in your offline data store. If you bring your network connection back to life, after a moment the offline message will disappear and your comment will be appended to the end of your comment list.

Congratulations, matey! You have a fully capable offline app!

Looking Ahead

Three chapters' worth of service workers is a lot, so next we'll shift a bit. There are things we can do with mobile web apps now that weren't possible just a few years ago. The next chapter will dive into what makes some of these features a reality: the *web app manifest.*

CHAPTER 6

Adding your App to the Home Screen with Web App Manifest

To this point, everything you've done could be applied to both a "traditional" web app you'd visit on your laptop or desktop computer as well as on a mobile device. In fact, offline capabilities are likely going to be needed more often on a mobile device than on a laptop. But the web app manifest is a PWA feature that is really mobile-focused. With it, you can specify details about your app that help devices give your users the best possible experience.

Because of this, you're going to be testing all of these features on an Android phone. If you don't have an Android phone, there are several emulators you can download to play around with to get Chrome installed and follow along.

Each thing I cover here really is best experienced on a device. For example, with a web app manifest, you can specify icons the device will use when a user saves your app to the home screen. You can specify visual themes and launch URLs and app names that show up under the app icon on a device home screen. There are options to change the browser's *chrome* to allow your app to appear as if it's not even running in a browser. And you can even specify a splash screen that launches as soon as your app does to avoid that couple of seconds of a blank white screen if you're fetching the app from the network instead of the cache.

© Dennis Sheppard 2017
D. Sheppard, *Beginning Progressive Web App Development*, https://doi.org/10.1007/978-1-4842-3090-9_6

Even better is that all of this is really easy and straightforward. You simply specify your options in a JSON file and reference it in your HTML files. Let's take a look at the manifest file you'll use:

```
{
  "name": "iPatch",
  "short_name": "iPatch",
  "start_url": "index.html",
  "display": "standalone",
  "theme_color": "#000",
  "background_color": "#000",
  "description": "The best pirate app on the high seas! Arrrgh!",
  "icons": [{
    "src": "images/app-icon48.png",
    "sizes": "48x48",
    "type": "image/png"
  }, {
    "src": "images/app-icon72.png",
    "sizes": "72x72",
    "type": "image/png"
  }, {
    "src": "images/app-icon96.png",
    "sizes": "96x96",
    "type": "image/png"
  }, {
    "src": "images/app-icon144.png",
    "sizes": "144x144",
    "type": "image/png"
  }, {
    "src": "images/app-icon168.png",
    "sizes": "168x168",
    "type": "image/png"
  }, {
    "src": "images/app-icon192.png",
    "sizes": "192x192",
    "type": "image/png"
```

```
}, {
  "src": "images/app-icon512.png",
  "sizes": "512x512",
  "type": "image/png"
}],
"prefer_related_applications": false,
"related_applications": [{
  "platform": "play",
  "url": "com.arrgh.pirates"
}],
"orientation": "portrait"
}
```

Most of this is self-explanatory, but Table 6-1 provides explanations just in case.

Table 6-1. *Web App Manifest Properties*

Property	Description
name	The name of your application. This will display under the app icon.
short_name	A fallback for the name, used anywhere the full name isn't.
start_url	The landing page for your users. Useful, for example, if your app is hosted on www.iheartpirates.com but you want your readers to go to www.iheartpirates.com/login.html when they launch.
display	Available display options are Fullscreen: Takes up the entire screen, and nothing of the web browser is visible. Probably preferred for games. Standalone: Most browser elements are hidden, like navigation, but some items might still show. minimal-ui: Essential UI elements of the browser are still visible, like navigation buttons. Browser: Just your normal old browser.
theme_color	Specifies what color to tint the browser elements, such as the browser's toolbar.
background_ color	Displays a color of your choosing as the background of your app before the style sheets have had an opportunity to load.

(*continued*)

Table 6-1. (*continued*)

Property	Description
description	Just what your app does.
icons	The icon of your app. Size: You can specify an icon size (even multiple sizes that are space-separated). It's important to include icons of different sizes as there are a variety of screen sizes your app should support Src: The path to the image. Type: The media type, so the browser can ignore the image if it doesn't support the file type
prefer_related_applications	You can specify related applications (in the next property), and this value tells the device OS to let the user know other applications are recommended over this one. That seems silly, but a good example of this is if your PWA is related to a native app that the user needs to perform a particular operation, and the feature just doesn't exist on the Web.
related_applications	A list of native applications related to your PWA. Could allow the browser to prompt a user to open the native version of your app.
orientation	Set your app to work only in landscape or only in portrait. You can also include any as a value, but this is the default.
dir	This is the text direction for the name, short_name, and description properties. By default, this will be ltr or "left to right," but for languages that are written right to left, put rtl here.
lang	This specifies the language for the name and short_name properties. This should be a string containing a single language. By default, this is 'en-US'.
scope	Much like the service worker scope from previous chapters, this property specifies which directories and files the web app manifest affects. This value should be a string representing a valid path of your application. If you don't specify this path, everything that is in the directory of the manifest and all subdirectories are included in the scope.

Now that I've covered what the manifest contains and what it does, you need to make sure you include it in your app. The following is just a one-liner to pop into each HTML page:

```
<link rel="manifest" href="manifest.json">
```

You have the manifest created, and you have it inside `index.html` and your other HTML pages. If you navigate to the app in Chrome and open DevTools, you can see the *Manifest* option on the left side of the *Application* tab like in Figure 6-1. In there, you have details about your app manifest and can even test the prompt to add your app to the home screen. So let's give it a shot.

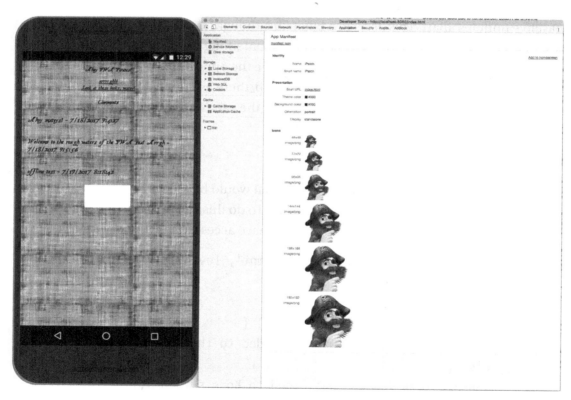

Figure 6-1. *App manifest details in DevTools*

Installing the App to the Home Screen

If you visit the page in Chrome on Android, it's still hitting your local dev server, so the pages won't be served over HTTPS. That is one of the requirements for Chrome to prompt a user to install your app to the home screen. Later on you'll deploy your app so that it will be served over HTTPS, and I'll go over how to run an HTTPS server locally. For now, you can use the *Add to Homescreen* button in DevTools to test the pop-up, which I'll talk about in just a moment.

The other criteria for Chrome prompting users to install your app are the name and short_name properties in your app manifest, a start_url *property that works while the user is offline*, a png icon that's at least 144px, and the user needs to visit the site twice, at least five minutes apart. This list is in a bit of flux, though, and is frequently updated. It's best to test your app frequently if this prompt is something that's important to you.

It's up to Chrome as to when the user will have the opportunity to respond to a prompt. However, when the prompt does show up, there are some things the browser will allow you to do to exercise more control over the user's experience.

Handling Installation Events

You may have analytics or other tracking tools that would be nice to use when it comes to how users respond to the installation prompt. To do this, you can listen to the beforeinstallprompt event anywhere that you have access to the window object:

```
window.addEventListener('beforeinstallprompt', (event) => {
    event.userChoice.then((result) => {
      console.log(result.outcome);
      if(result.outcome === 'dismissed') {
        console.log('The app was not added to the home screen');
      } else {
        console.log('The app was added to home screen');
      }
    });
  });
```

Once the event fires, the userChoice object on the event returns a promise with the result. From there you can check whether the user dismissed the installation dialog.

Additionally, you can stop the prompt from happening and store it to display to the user at a later time. This is useful because users tend to be wary about pop-ups and prompts to do things. So it's a best practice to show the prompt once the user either asks for it or has a positive experience with your app, rather than seemingly randomly asking them to add the app to the homescreen. You can do that by calling event.preventDefault(); and assigning the event to a variable for later usage:

```
var deferredPrompt;
window.addEventListener('beforeinstallprompt', (event) => {
    event.preventDefault();
    deferredPrompt = event;
});
document.getElementById('install-to-home-screen').addEventListener('click',
() => {
  if(deferredPrompt) {
    deferredPrompt.prompt();
    deferredPrompt.userChoice.then((result) => {
      console.log(result.outcome);
      if(result.outcome === 'dismissed') {
        console.log('The app was not added to the home screen');
      } else {
        console.log('The app was added to home screen');
      }
    });
    delete deferredPrompt;
  }
});
```

Manually Adding the App to the Home Screen

Of course, all of this assumes Chrome prompts the user, which is not guaranteed. Luckily for us devs, we can test adding the app to the home screen via DevTools (*see Figure* 6-1) and users can manually add the app to their home screen from Chrome's menu, shown in Figure 6-2.

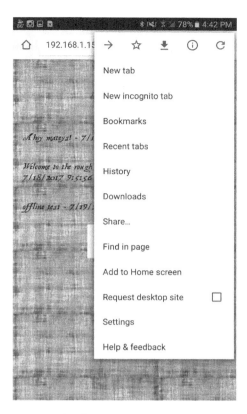

Figure 6-2. *Adding the app to the home screen*

If you launch the app, you can go ahead and tap *Add to Home screen.* Like in Figure 6-3, Chrome will present you with a pop-up showing your app icon and an input box pre-filled with the name of the app. Users are welcome to change the name to whatever they'd like.

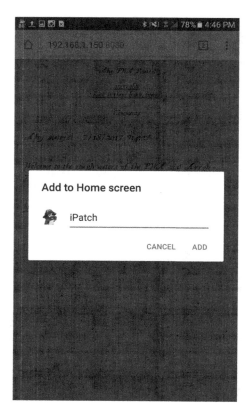

Figure 6-3. *Icon and name of app*

Once the user chooses a name and taps *ADD*, Figure 6-4 shows how the app gets added to the home screen.

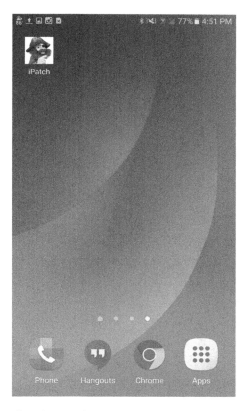

Figure 6-4. *The app on the device home screen*

This is fantastic! Your app is available for launching right there on the device. It is worth noting, however, that the app really is just on the home screen. If you go looking for it in the app drawer, you're not going to find it.

The App Splash Screen

In the early days of having web apps launchable from an icon on the home screen, the experience was fairly janky. The user would launch and see a white screen for several seconds before any content was visible. Now, of course, you've cached everything, and your app loads very quickly. But in case of super slow connections, or if you're less aggressive in your caching, Chrome has the ability to show the user a splash screen at launch, rather than just waiting for content to load. The best part about the splash screen is that it's automatically shown based on properties you've already put in your app manifest.

The splash screen is generated from name, background_color, and the icon in the list of icons that is closest to 128dp, with a minimum of 48dp for the icon to show.

Note   If the dp is a unit you're not familiar with, 1dp is the same thing as 1px on a screen with a density of 160dpi. The Samsung Galaxy S7, for example, has a dpi of 576. So an image of 128dp would need to be a 460px image. In the example manifest, the highest resolution image is 192px. This is the equivalent of 53dp. That's on the small side, but workable for this particular device. Anything smaller than 192px, though, and Lighthouse will penalize you!

Now that you have your PWA added to the home screen of the device, go ahead and launch the app using the icon. As it launches, you should see your app icon with the *name* of the app right below it, along with the background color specified in the app manifest, just like in Figure 6-5.

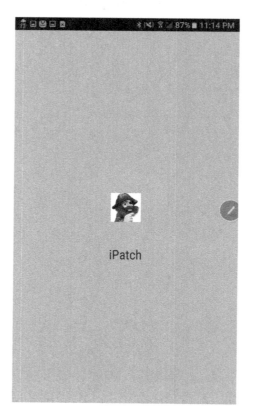

Figure 6-5. *Splash screen*

The display Property

The `display` property in the example app manifest is set to `fullscreen`, which means that none of the web browser will show. That means your PWA will look like a native app to the user. In this case, the Pirate App is "designed" (using the word in the loosest sense) to look like a web app, not a mobile app. But if your app has a very mobile look and feel, getting rid of the browser chrome around the app will really give the app a native feel. Take a look at Figure 6-6 to see what a PWA would look like on a mobile device without any browser chrome.

Note   When referring to the "chrome" of the browser, this is not a reference to the Chrome browser. Instead, a browser's chrome consists of its visible features, such as the address bar, navigation buttons, menu options, etc.

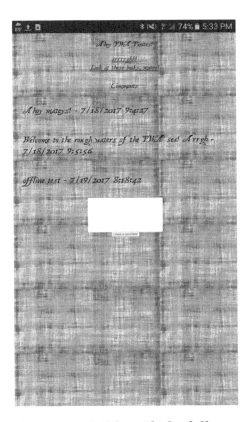

Figure 6-6. *No browser chrome is visible with the fullscreen option*

Note If you try making changes to your app manifest, make sure to clear out your mobile device's browsing data. Remember, you're caching a lot of things now, so it can be frustrating when you make a change and don't see it reflected in the app. Most of the time, simply clearing browser data and opening the app in a new tab will do the trick. Also, when testing changes having to do with adding the app to the home screen, don't forget to delete the app you have already added to the home screen.

Try a few different settings for `display` to see which one you prefer for your app.

The start_url Property

You initially set the `start_url` of the manifest to `index.html`, which is the default main entry point of your app anyway. Feel free to tweak that to other pages of the app to see that the app launches to the set `start_url`. This seems like a small feature, but think of the flexibility this affords developers for web apps. With the combination of a fullscreen display, a different manifest with a different start URL, your PWA could actually consist of numerous apps. Maybe you want an app dedicated solely to pirate books. In that case, you could reference a different manifest on `pirate_books.html` with a `start_url` of `pirate_books.html` so that when a user installs it with no browser chrome, the entire app consists of just that page. That's pretty powerful for a simple old web app.

It's also possible to track certain metrics in your PWA by adding query string params to the `start_url`. With that, you can track whether a user installed your PWA and when and how often the app is launched.

Looking Ahead

You're now able to bring your apps closer and closer to their native counterparts. Your apps work offline, load super-fast with the cache, and users can launch them from the home screen. Next, I'll talk about giving your users the capability to stay engaged with a web app like never before by using push notifications.

CHAPTER 7

Notifications

This chapter is going to cover something that has become a little bit controversial recently. While push notifications on the Web are a powerful feature that inches the Web ever closer to native apps, some developers have started to transform them into trite annoyances that have conditioned users to ignore notifications or turn them off outright. How often do you give an app the okay to send you notifications on your phone? On the Web? There's a good chance you're pretty stingy with which apps you give permission to send you notifications. So before we dive in to the technical aspects of this feature, let's examine the responsibility that will be bestowed upon you.

Imagine, if you will, that you walk into a store. Maybe it's a clothing store or a grocery store, doesn't matter. And the second you walk in the door, an employee of the establishment is in your face, asking if he or she can call you regularly. Or text you. Or mail you something or even show up at your house.

Best case, you'll try a nifty spin move to get around this crazy person and get to the shopping you desire. Worst case, you're going to turn around and just leave the store.

No one wants to be harassed in this way. Perhaps you think this is overstating the problem. A push notification never hurt anyone, right? True, but they can be a nuisance, and a good way to drive away users if they're not done correctly. As an example, just in doing some research about this very topic, you might run across a site that looks like Figure 7-1.

© Dennis Sheppard 2017

D. Sheppard, *Beginning Progressive Web App Development*, https://doi.org/10.1007/978-1-4842-3090-9_7

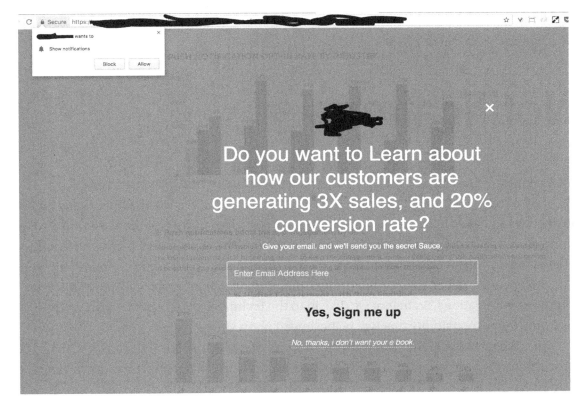

Figure 7-1. *Overly aggressive engagement attempts—pretty meta*

Within seconds of arriving on this page (that shall remain unidentified), the user is bombarded with a request for notifications and to sign up for a newsletter. Take it easy, site; we just met! If you haven't even had a chance to show users what your app is or what it's offering them, there's very little chance a user is going to automatically sign up for your notifications.

I could talk about opt-in statistics by industry and platform, and that Android users are more likely to allow an app to send push notifications than iOS, or that both numbers are declining in general. I could talk about engagement rates and how they go up once a user does accept push notifications. But all of those stats miss the point that waiting for the right opportunity to ask your users if they would like you to send them notifications is the real key. And that opportunity is not the very second they land on your page!

The opportunity will vary from app to app. Ideally, though, you'll want to wait until the user has done something that indicates an interest in whatever the push notifications

are about. Maybe you even wait for the user to click a big button that says *Enable Push Notifications*. Whatever the opportunity is, remember to treat your users how you'd like to be treated.

Now that the PSA portion of the chapter is out of the way, let's look at how you might (responsibly) engage with your users via notifications!

Web Notifications

This chapter will cover two different types of notifications: *web notifications* and *push notifications*. The former is done entirely using front-end code, with no need for a server to be involved. If a user has your app open on a desktop browser, web notifications are a possible option. If, however, you need to send your user a notification even when the browser tab is closed or the device is in a pocket, push notifications are your only option. They originate from a server and use a web notification to notify the user even if the app isn't active.

Of course, while the "push" flavor of notifications is more powerful, it also is quite a bit more complex. So let's start with web notifications to ease our way in here.

Requesting Permission to Notify

What would a pirate app be without a parrot? So Figure 7-2 introduces... Peggy the Parrot!

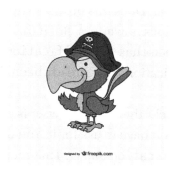

Figure 7-2. *Say hi to Peggy the Parrot.*

111

Peggy gets hungry a lot, and once you visit her, it's your responsibility to feed her. It'd be helpful if you got a notification reminding you to feed her, lest she get cranky and fly away. If that happened, you might have to walk the plank for losing the Captain's bird. So let's create that notification:

```
document.addEventListener('DOMContentLoaded', initPage, false);
function initPage() {
  if (!('Notification' in window)) {
    // this browser does not support notifications
  } else if (Notification.permission === 'denied') {
    // the user denied notification permission!
  } else if (Notification.permission === 'granted') {
    // setup UI to show notifications already enabled
  }

  notificationsBtn.addEventListener('click', () => {
    Notification.requestPermission();
  });
}
```

Create a peggy_parrot.html file, or download the repo from the Chapter7-example-1_web_notifications branch. You can just tuck your script into that file for now.

Once the DOM is finished loading, you can get started with your initPage function. You want to check a few things first. Does this browser support notifications? Just about every modern desktop browser does nowadays. But if this user's doesn't, you can display a message when you check if window has the Notification object. You also can go ahead and check if permission for notifications has already been denied or granted, and you can adjust the UI accordingly.

If after making the initial checks the user's browser is good to go, and permission hasn't been granted or denied, you have to ask for it. You do that by calling requestPermission on the Notification object. That method returns a promise, so if you want to do anything after permission is granted, this is the place. For now, you don't need anything in there, so you'll leave the then function off.

Sending a Notification

Next, go ahead and create your function that sends a notification to the browser:

```
function sendNotification(opacityRemaining) {
  let options = {
    body: 'Peggy wants a pretzel! You have ' + (opacityRemaining * 10 * 3)
    + ' seconds to feed her!',
    icon: 'images/peggy_parrot.jpg'
  };

  let notification = new Notification('Peggy says', options);
}
```

Notifications take an `options` object. The `options` object has a lot of properties you could set on it, including an `icon` the notification can display, `actions` (which is an array of actions the user has to interact with the notification), `body` for text the notification displays, `vibrate` (which allows a vibration pattern on mobile devices), and a lot more. For now, you're going to keep things simple and just have an icon and body text. Feel free to experiment with some of the other notification option properties. You can find a list of all of them here: `https://developer.mozilla.org/docs/Web/API/Notification/Notification`.

To send the notification, you just make a new `Notification` object, passing in a `title` (which is just a string) and your `options` object. You can do some things with the `Notification` object that is returned, such as closing it after a certain amount of time, or listen for events about the notification such as an error if the notification couldn't sent for some reason or a click event if the user interacts with the notification. But it's not required to do anything with that returned object.

The `opacityRemaining` variable is linked to how hungry Peggy is before she disappears. Let's go ahead and make Peggy the Parrot hungry. That will be represented symbolically by having Peggy fade from the user's view over 30 seconds. When Peggy is halfway faded, you should notify the user that they need to feed the bird. Feeding the

bird, in this case, simply consists of the user pressing a button that resets the bird image's opacity to 1.0:

```
function makeParrotHungry() {
  let parrotPic = document.getElementById('parrot');
  let interval = setInterval(() => {
    parrotPic.style.opacity -= .1;
    if (parrotPic.style.opacity <= 0) {
      clearInterval(interval);
      // Peggy has flown away to find food
    } else if (parrotPic.style.opacity < .5) {
      sendNotification(+parrotPic.style.opacity);
    }
  }, 1000 * 3);
}

function feedParrot() {
  let parrotPic = document.getElementById('parrot');
  parrotPic.style.opacity = 1.0;
}
```

Every three seconds, you decrement the opacity on the image by .1. When the opacity gets under .5, you want to send the browser a notification, so call the sendNotification function. To display how many seconds the user has to feed Peggy, you have to pass sendNotification the remaining opacity. If the opacity gets down to zero, you can clear out the interval because by that point, it's too late. The bird has abandoned you from lack of love and care.

To get this going, you need the image of the parrot in your HTML view, along with a button to enable notifications and a button to feed Peggy:

```
<button id="enable-notifications">Enable Notifications</button>
<img src="images/peggy_parrot.jpg" id="parrot">
<button id="feed-parrot">Feed Peggy</button>
```

Go ahead and run this if you've been typing along or you've pulled down the branch Chapter7-example-1_web_notifications from github.com/dennissheppard/pwa. If you're simply typing along, that branch has some items you might need, like the picture of Peggy and a couple of other assets. You could also apply something similar to your

own app. When you load the `peggy_parrot.html` page, you should see our beautiful bird. Wait a few seconds, and you'll get a notification! Depending on your OS, the notification should look something like Figure 7-3.

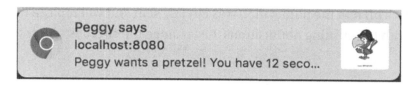

Figure 7-3. *Notification you created letting you know to feed Peggy*

This is pretty great. That's all it took to get a notification.

But wait another few seconds, and you'll see your notification change to 9 and then another few seconds 6, etc. Because you send a notification on every interval once the opacity reaches a certain point, you're getting a little bit clogged up.

Imagine if you had an app that sent a notification every time a new message arrived. If your user is a popular person, all of those notifications could stack up really quickly. Take Figure 7-4, for example.

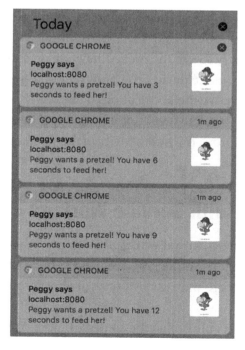

Figure 7-4. *Notifications stacking up!*

Tagging Notifications

To alleviate this problem, you can use the tag property. The tag property should contain any string that you would like to identify a notification. When you tag a notification, the browser will pick up that the notification was already sent and will replace the older notifications with the ensuing notifications. Just change the options object to include a tag property:

```
function sendNotification(opacityRemaining) {
  let options = {
    body: 'Peggy wants a pretzel! You have ' + (opacityRemaining * 10 * 3)
+ ' seconds to feed her!',
    icon: 'images/peggy_parrot.jpg',
    tag: 'feed-peggy'
  };

  let notification = new Notification('Peggy says', options);
}
```

Now if you neglect to feed Peggy, you should see just the most recent notification. This is great for the Web, but pretty basic. The biggest drawback is that this will only work on desktop browsers. If you try to run the preceding code on a mobile device, you're not going to get anything. On a mobile device, the browser tab won't stay active to notify you. Instead, you'd need to move the notification to the service worker level. You knew service workers were going to get involved sooner or later! Let's take a look at how you'd do this and how you can improve the interactivity of the push notification to help your users feed Peggy.

Web Notifications with Service Workers

When you get service workers involved with notifications, they're called *persistent notifications*. It really just means you're going to use a service worker to handle your notifications. Service workers remain persistent in the background of the app, whether it's running or not.

Almost all of your code is going to be the same as before. You'll just tweak the line that actually sends the notification in the sendNotification function and add an actions property to the options object:

```
function sendNotification(secondsLeft) {
  let options = {
    body: 'Peggy wants a pretzel! You have ' + (secondsLeft * 10 * 3) + '
    seconds to feed her!',
    icon: 'images/peggy_parrot.jpg',
    actions: [
      {
        action: "feed", title: "Feed Peggy"
      },
      {
        action: "wait", title: "Wait to Feed Peggy"
      }
    ]
  };

    navigator.serviceWorker.ready.then((sw) => {
      sw.showNotification('Peggy says', options);
    });
}
```

First, let's look at that `actions` property. You have an array with two objects in it. Both have an `action` property and a `title` property. The `action` property is essentially an ID that you'll use to know if the user clicked that action. The `title` property is the text you'll show the user.

Note   The `actions` property is currently quite limited in its browser support. Only Chrome supports it. If you'd like to use it, make sure it's a progressive enhancement, and that your entire app doesn't rely on it.

The next change is at the bottom of the function. You need to wait until the service worker is ready, and once it is, you can call `showNotification` on the registration object passed in via the promise, called `sw`. Other than that, it's the same idea.

You'll actually be able to listen for user interaction events on the notification so that you can detect if a user selected *Feed Peggy* or *Wait to Feed Peggy*. You listen for those in the service worker, though, and since you'll need the service worker to set up your whole push notification feature, let's circle back to listening for those events.

Push Notifications

Now that you've laid some groundwork for notifications by requesting permission, sending a notification from the browser, and setting up some actions for use while wiring up the service worker, you can get down into the weeds of push notifications. As mentioned, these notifications originate from a server, so the browser doesn't even need to be open to receive these notifications.

The process (also viewable in Figure 7-5) in which this works is as follows:

1. After the user grants permission to receive notifications, the app asks a web push service for a `PushSubscription` object. Each browser is in charge of implementing that web push service. You don't particularly care what that service is, as long as you can request a `PushSubscription` and it returns one.

2. The web push service returns the `PushSubscription` object to the browser.

3. The app sends the `PushSubscription` object to your app server for safe keeping.

4. When some action requires a push notification, the app server tells the web push service to send a notification based on a set of keys (more about those in a bit).

5. The web push service sends the notification to the browser, where it's handled by the service worker.

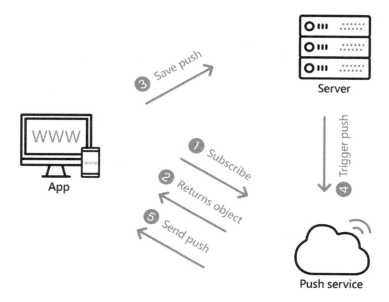

Figure 7-5. *Push notification architecture*

That's a lot of steps, but I'll make sure to cover each one. As mentioned, however, this part does get significantly more complex. Here be dragons.

Subscribing a User to Push Notifications

To send a push message to a user, you need a PushSubscription object from the browser. That object contains all the information the server needs to identify your browser and send a push message. So as soon as you get the PushSubscription object, you can send it off to your own server, and the battle is half won. Let's go over how to subscribe the user.

The first thing you need are Voluntary Application Server Identification (VAPID) keys, also known as application server keys. This is a set of alphanumeric strings that identifies your application on the web push server. Using them, the server will know who is requesting the push and who will receive it. This is a security precaution to make sure there's nothing iniquitous happening between the application and the server, such as the push service reading message data rather than it being private to the end user or someone sending you push notifications that shouldn't be. Imagine spam push notifications... Yuck.

This set of keys contains a public key and a private key, one that you can share, another that you shouldn't. You can generate a set of keys a couple of different ways, but the easiest is by visiting `https://web-push-codelab.appspot.com/`. This is a site created by Google and is pretty self-explanatory. Just hit the *Refresh Keys* button to get a public and private key. Keep that page open, because you're about to use the public key.

In `pirate-manager.js`, let's throw the public key at the top of the file and assign it to a variable called `publicServerKey`. Then add a reference to a method you'll call `subscribeToPush`. Then you just need to create that method to subscribe the user to push notifications.

```
var publicServerKey =
'BIPFAXHI5YOZQFIU4bUyyKgKxqPWJJMf7WHZkMg1u7XeljjeNpwad5fvJXwtbOEN7
cvEA_6pzwjYsY9_gLQFnRs';

return {
  getComments: getComments,
  postComment: postComment,
  registerServiceWorker: registerServiceWorker,
  subscribeToPush: subscribeToPush
  };

......

function subscribeToPush() {
    const options = {
      userVisibleOnly: true,
      applicationServerKey: urlB64ToUint8Array(publicServerKey)
    };
    navigator.serviceWorker.ready.then((reg) => {
      return reg.pushManager.subscribe(options);
    })
    .then((subscription) => {
      console.log('subscription: ', JSON.stringify(subscription));
      return subscription;
    });
  }
```

```
function urlB64ToUint8Array(base64String) {
  const padding = '='.repeat((4 - base64String.length % 4) % 4);
  const base64 = (base64String + padding)
    .replace(/\-/g, '+')
    .replace(/_/g, '/');

  const rawData = window.atob(base64);
  const outputArray = new Uint8Array(rawData.length);

  for (let i = 0; i < rawData.length; ++i) {
    outputArray[i] = rawData.charCodeAt(i);
  }
  return outputArray;
}
```

Let's get that 600lb gorilla out of the way. That `urlB64ToUint8Array` function is ridiculous. Don't even look at it. Okay, fine, take 10 seconds because you know you're going to. Done? Alright, yes, it's ridiculous, and it's borrowed directly from Google's push notifications repo on GitHub: `https://github.com/GoogleChrome/push-notifications/blob/master/app/scripts/main.js`. You need it because the push subscription needs the public server key as a UInt8Array. So you'll use that function to get it into the appropriate format and be on your way. Thanks, Google!

Looking above that crazy function, the `subscribeToPush` method has an `options` object. One of the options is `userVisibleOnly`, which has to be set to `true` and has to be included. There was a plan once upon a time to allow devs to send users silent push notifications in case they wanted to update the app or do something without bothering the user with a visible notification. A sneaky dev could use that for shady purposes, so for now only visible pushes are allowed.

Note   That silent push notifications plan is now encompassed in the Budget API, which allows limited background work without notifying the user, like a silent push notification. Each site will be given a "budget" of resources to use to limit how much happens in the background without the user being notified.

The next option is your `applicationServerKey` that you're converting. Once you have them, you need a reference to your service worker registration object that has access to the `pushManager` that has a `subscribe` method on it. You pass in your options and wait for a successful then that should have your `PushSubscription` object.

Note   You may be wondering what actually happens in that `subscribe` method on the `pushManager`. The browser is making a call to a push service with your public server key to register your app with an endpoint. That endpoint will be returned to you in the `PushSubscription` object. Each browser has a different push service, but lucky for us the API is all the same. The only thing you need concern yourself with is sending off your key to the `subscribe` method.

Add a call to `pirateManager.subscribeToPush` in the peggy_parrot script on the check to see if notifications have been enabled. That way if the user had granted permission on a previous page load, you can just subscribe to push right away. If permission wasn't granted before, you want to make a call to subscribe to them down in the `enableNotifications` function.

```
document.addEventListener('DOMContentLoaded', initPage, false);
  function initPage() {
    if (!('Notification' in window)) {
      // this browser does not support notifications
    } else if (Notification.permission === 'denied') {
      // the user denied notification permission!
    else if (Notification.permission === 'granted') {
      pirateManager.subscribeToPush();
    }

...

function enableNotifications() {
  Notification.requestPermission().then((result) => {
    pirateManager.subscribeToPush();
  });
}
```

You can go ahead and run this, and if you have DevTools open, you should see something like Figure 7-6.

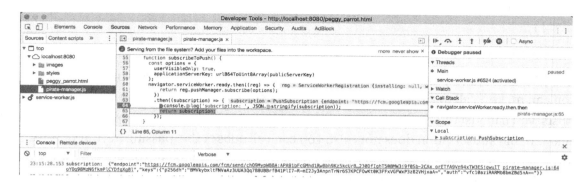

Figure 7-6. *PushSubscription returned from subscribe call*

Slaying these dragons one step at a time. You can now check to see if your user has a subscription before making a call to subscribe:

```
function subscribeToPush() {
  const options = {
    userVisibleOnly: true,
    applicationServerKey: urlB64ToUint8Array(publicServerKey)
  };
  navigator.serviceWorker.ready.then((reg) => {
      return reg.pushManager.getSubscription().then((subscription) => {
        if (subscription === null) {
          return reg.pushManager.subscribe(options);
        } else {
          let promise = new Promise((resolve, reject) => {
            resolve(subscription);
          });
          return promise;
        }
      });
    })
```

```
    .then((subscription) => {
      console.log('subscription: ', JSON.stringify(subscription));
      return subscription;
    });
}
```

When you get your registration object once you check if the service worker is ready, you can make a call to getSubscription on the pushManager object. If the subscription exists, you can just return that in your own promise; you don't need to subscribe the user again. If that subscription does not exist, you can call subscribe, passing in your options just like before. In either case, you will still hit the then function at the bottom of the code snippet with a subscription object passed in.

Note   Checking if the user is already subscribed is also good practice so that you can update your UI accordingly. For example, if you have a button asking the user to subscribe to push notifications, checking beforehand can allow you to disable the button or let the user know they're already subscribed.

Saving the PushSubscription Object

Your next step is to save that subscription information on your own back-end server. You might be thinking, *I don't have a server*. You're right. You don't have a server. Now what? Build one?

You'll be using a very simple Express server to handle your server-side push notifications. If you haven't worked with Express before, don't panic. Don't let your eyes gloss over. Just another dragon to slay.

To get a full understanding of what's happening with push notifications, try to follow along with the server-side code. There are a few parts that are particularly relevant to push notifications that will be called out. If you'd really like, though, you can ignore most of this server-side code and just use this file. When it comes time to implement push notifications on your own projects, though, the pattern and steps will largely be the same, but there is logic specific to the pirate app. Just change the endpoints to whatever you need, and update the timing of when you want the push notifications to show.

First, in your terminal run, type

```
npm install --save express web-push body-parser
```

This will install your necessary libraries, including *web-push*. That's a library that's going to make your life significantly easier by handling all of the necessary authentication and security protocols with the VAPID keys.

Now, create a directory in the root of your app and call it `server`. Inside there, create a blank JavaScript file. You'll use `server.js` in this project, but feel free to call it whatever you'd like. I'm going to cover what goes in that file in chunks so it's not too overwhelming.

```
let express = require("express");
let webPush = require('web-push');
let bodyParser = require('body-parser');
let app = express();
let subscriptions = [];
let timeLeft = 15;
let timer;
```

At the top of the file, declare some variables. You need to bring in both ExpressJS and the web-push libraries. You also need to bring in a package that allows you to grab the body of whatever you post to your server's endpoints. That's what the `body-parser` package does.

You create an instance of Express, an array that will hold your `PushSubscription` objects, and then some variables to deal with the timing for how long it takes Peggy to fade out.

If you were really setting this up to be accurate, most of the logic for managing Peggy's state would live on the server. As it stands, the logic is a little spread out and leads to some inconsistencies that you'll see. But for the purposes of push notifications, you just need to know when to show them. So I've moved just enough logic to the server to be able to handle that.

```
app.use(bodyParser.json());
app.use(function(req, res, next) {
  res.header("Access-Control-Allow-Origin", "*");
  res.header("Access-Control-Allow-Headers", "Origin, X-Requested-With,
Content-Type, Accept");
  next();
});
```

Here you're telling your Express app to use the body parser. Then you need to add in a block of code for cross-origin resource sharing (CORS). This allows you to hit your API from a different domain. You need that because your server will be running on a different port than the front end of your code. You don't have to set it up this way. If you'd like, Express can serve all of your front-end code as well. For now, though, you're sticking with your original dev server for the front end, and Express will live one port higher. You'll see that code in a bit.

```
const vapidKeys = {
  publicKey:
'BCi3AfGJVfxoDOB3JGMbvyAzOBJ8KiqRrUn6OhYaWsfUrwOq6h9hI1x464AQaVyaNFhAGNio
thYCtSxRmyOP8SI',
  privateKey: 'tjl2sNdpoiLYqUhR_TjSSZNq1U2fcBNw2LT76C_nCOM'
};

webPush.setVapidDetails(
  'mailto:dennissheppard+pwa@gmail.com',
  vapidKeys.publicKey,
  vapidKeys.privateKey
);
```

Here is a code block that's particularly relevant to push notifications. Remember those VAPID keys you created? You need to send those off to the web-push library. You also have to include some kind of link that includes a *mailto* email address in case the third-party push server needs to contact whomever is sending the messages:

```
app.post('/register', (req, res) => {
  if (!req.body || !req.body.endpoint) {
    // Invalid subscription.
    res.status(400);
    res.send('Invalid subscription');
    return false;
  }

  console.log('Subscription registered ' + req.body.endpoint);
  const found = subscriptions.some((sub) => {
    return sub.endpoint === req.body.endpoint;
```

```
  });
  if (!found) {
    subscriptions.push(req.body);
  }

  if (!timer) {
    setPushTimer();
  }

  res.sendStatus(200);
});
```

Here's another section that's pertinent to notifications. Remember that you have to save your subscription on the server? This is the main part of step three in the overall architecture from Figure 7-5.

This chunk of code sets up an endpoint with which you can POST that subscription to from the front end. The route to the endpoint is just /register, and it will take your pushSubscription object on the body of the POST. That object needs to have the endpoint property on it so the push server knows where to send the notification. If any of that stuff is bad, you return a 400 error telling the front end that the subscription is invalid.

If everything went well, you will want to add the subscription object to your array of subscriptions. There's some code in there to ensure you're not saving duplicate subscriptions. In your production apps, you'll likely want to save that subscription to a database for future sessions, but let's stay focused on the task at hand here.

After saving the subscription in your array, if you haven't already set the timer in motion, you do so with setPushTimer(). Let's look at that function next:

```
function setPushTimer() {
  timer = setTimeout(() => {
    console.log('timeleft: ', timeLeft);
    subscriptions.forEach(sendNotification);
  }, 1000 * timeLeft);
}
```

This is pirate app-specific logic. After a certain amount of time, you want to send the notification. In your case, it's about half-way through the time it takes Peggy to fade out. In your apps, that logic will be up to whatever rules you have to show the notifications. For this app, it's a simple timeout. Once the timeout executes, you want to send the notification for each subscription you have. Again, this will vary depending on the app.

Now, let's look at what it takes to actually send that notification.

Triggering the Push Notification

This is the code that will actually send the notification to the push server, which will then contact your browser. This is step four and five of the flow we went over before. Step five is taken care of for you by the web-push library and the push server, but triggering all of that is up to you.

```
function sendNotification(subscription) {
  timer = null;
  const notificationText = 'Peggy wants a pretzel! You have ' + timeLeft + '
seconds to feed her!';
  webPush.sendNotification(subscription, notificationText).then(function() {
    console.log('Notification sent');
  }).catch(function(error) {
    console.log('Error sending Notification' + error);
    subscriptions.splice(subscriptions.indexOf(endpoint), 1);
  });
}
```

Once you're ready to send the notification, you can kill your timer. Then, whatever data you want to send with the push notification along with your subscription object you passed in to this function is included in a sendNotification method on the webPush object. That returns a promise you can use to do something after the notification was sent or to handle errors. In your case, if for some reason the notification didn't send, the subscription is no good, so you want to remove that subscription object from your array of them.

At this point, your notification is sent! The cycle is complete.

You're not quite done yet, though. What happens when or if the user feeds Peggy? You need to reset the timer and notify them again later. So you need something that the front end can use to update that timer. Again, this is an item that's really specific to this

particular app, but you'll see later how you can use the following logic to enable users to interact directly with notifications:

```
app.post('/feed', (req, res) => {
  timeLeft = 15;
  if (!timer) {
    setPushTimer();
  }
  res.sendStatus(200);
});
```

This is a very simple endpoint the front end can POST to that resets the timer. This way if the user does feed Peggy, you can send off another notification when she's hungry again:

```
app.listen(8081, function() {
  console.log(`Listening on port 8081`);
});
```

The last thing you need to do on your server is just start it up. As mentioned, you're running it one port above where your front-end server is running, but configure your ports and where your server is running however you'd like.

To get the server running, go to a new terminal window or tab, navigate to the root of your app and run

```
node server/server.js
```

and you should see something like in Figure 7-7.

Figure 7-7. *When you run the server, it should let you know that it's running and listening on whatever port you configured it to use*

Now that the server is running, you can hit one of your new endpoints to make sure the timer is resetting when you feed Peggy. So you need to hop back over to the front end to update your `feedParrot` function inside `peggy_parrot.html`:

```
function feedParrot() {
  let parrotPic = document.getElementById('parrot');
  parrotPic.style.opacity = 1.0;
  fetch('http://localhost:8081/feed', {
    method: 'post'
  }).then(() => {
    console.log('fed and posted');
  });
}
```

The front-end code should now be hitting your locally running API, though you may need to change the URL in the `fetch` call to your local IP address instead of `localhost`. Once that's in, whenever the user clicks the Feed Peggy button, the server will be updated to reset the timer that controls when a push notification will show.

And that's it for the server! If you'd never worked with Express or node before, you're basically an expert now. Time to move back to the service worker, because you need to catch those notifications that the push server is now sending your way. And remember, these will notify the browser even if your particular app was closed. What makes that possible is your wonderful service worker. Let's take a look!

Catching Push Events in the Service Worker

Your service worker is the part of your app that will handle displaying the push notifications when it receives the push event from the push server. That means all of the notification logic will live in the service worker and run when it receives the event:

```
self.addEventListener('push', function(event) {
  console.log(`Push received with this data: "${event.data.text()}"`);

  const title = 'Peggy says:';

  let options = {
    body: event.data.text(),
```

```
  icon: 'images/peggy_parrot.jpg',
  actions: [
    {
      action: "feed", title: "Feed Peggy"
    },
    {
      action: "wait", title: "Wait to Feed Peggy"
    }
  ]
};


  event.waitUntil(self.registration.showNotification(title, options));
});
```

When you catch the push event, you have your familiar options object with your icon and actions and body. Before, you were configuring that body text on the front end. You can still do that if you'd like, but this example shows that you can just as easily display text that you sent from your server. You can configure the server to send other data too, but in your case it is a simple text string you want in the body of the notification.

You don't want the push event to end until you've had a chance to actually show the notification. So you throw your showNotification method inside the event.waitUntil function. showNotification lives on the self.registration object and requires your title and the options object, which is how you've been showing notifications all along.

You're finally ready to run all this code! Your server should already be running. Make sure your front-end server is still going. At this point, it'd probably be helpful to clear out anything from before. In DevTools in the *Application* tab, there's an option to clear application data (see Figure 7-8). Let's do that and make sure you don't have anything cached that would mess us up.

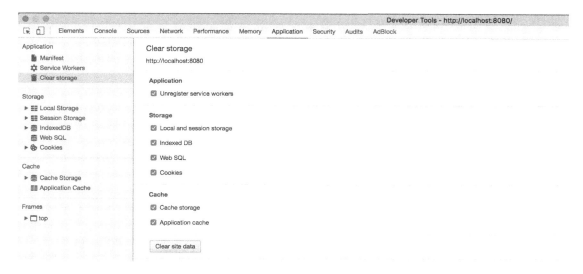

Figure 7-8. *Clearing application data*

When this runs, navigate to the `peggy_parrot.html` page. If the button is visible, enabling you to show notifications, do so and accept permission. If you've done that previously, it's likely that the button won't be there.

Wait about 15 seconds (or however long you set the timer for in `server.js` code) and you should see a notification. It will look different depending on your OS, but not only should you see a notification, but you'll also have options with which to interact with the notification, like in Figure 7-9.

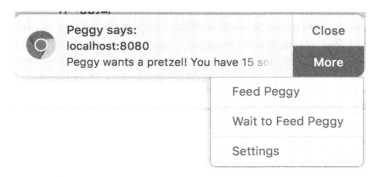

Figure 7-9. *Notification from the server with action options*

In fact, you should even be able to close the browser tab and *still* see the notification!

Maybe even more impressively, you can turn off your phone's screen in that 15-second window and receive the notification there as well, but not before setting up the ability to connect an Android device to the dev server via port forwarding.

Testing Push on Mobile

As previously discussed, service workers are only allowed on secure connections. The exception to that is for using `localhost`. You can hit your development server from a mobile device (if both are on the same internal network) by using the IP address, but unless you set up TLS for your dev server, the service worker isn't going to install when you run your app on mobile.

The good news is that the desktop version of Chrome allows you to set up remote debugging for your Android device by using port forwarding.

Connect your Android to your computer using a USB cable. On your Android device, make sure the connection mode isn't set to *Charge Only*. You may be presented with a list of options on your device that looks like Figure 7-10.

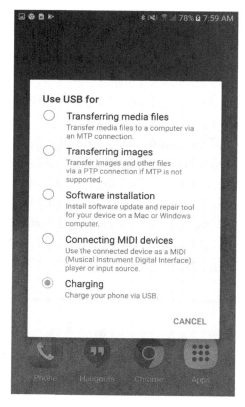

Figure 7-10. *Changing your Android connection from Charge Only*

Either of the *Transferring* options will work.

Now open DevTools on Chrome and at the bottom next to the console, you should see an option that says *Remote Devices*, as in Figure 7-11.

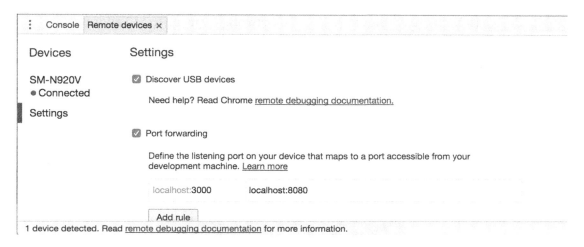

Figure 7-11. *Remote devices option on DevTools*

In *Settings*, you'll see a an option that says *Port forwarding*. Click *Add rule* and in the left textbox, enter whatever port you'd like to use on your Android device to connect to your dev server. This example uses port 3000, but put in whatever you'd like. In the right textbox, enter the address you would like Android to connect to when you use `localhost:3000`. In your case, that's the machine's localhost on port 8080.

Now you should be able to open a Chrome tab on Android, navigate to localhost:3000, and you're hitting your dev server's localhost:8080. The service worker will install, and everything should work as expected, with a push notification on the mobile device, just like in Figure 7-12.

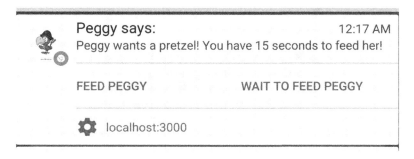

Figure 7-12. *Push notification on mobile*

Your last step is to enable those buttons on the notification to actually do something. For that, you turn to your trusty service worker.

Handling Notification Click Events

Just like you listened for the push event in the service worker, so too can you listen to a notificationclicked event. And because you put the action property on your actions array on the notification options, you can also know if the user clicked on one of the buttons or anywhere else. This gives you a lot of flexibility depending on what you want your app to do or what purpose you want your notifications to serve. In this case, you can feed Peggy without ever having to open your application. Let's see how:

```
self.addEventListener("notificationclick", (event) => {
  let promise = new Promise((resolve) => {
    event.notification.close();
    if (event.action === "feed") {
        fetch('http://localhost:8081/feed', {
          method: 'post',
          headers: {
            'Accept': 'application/json',
            'Content-Type': 'application/json'
          }
        }).then(() => resolve());
    } else if (event.action !== 'wait') {
      self.clients.matchAll().then((clients) => {
        if (clients.length > 0) {
          clients[0].navigate("http://localhost:8080/peggy_parrot.
          html?feed=true");
        } else {
          self.clients.openWindow("http://localhost:8080/peggy_parrot.
          html?feed=true");
        }
```

```
        resolve();
      });
    }
  });
  event.waitUntil(promise);
});
```

In the service worker, you listen for the notificationClick event. Because you don't want that event to finish until you're done with everything, at the bottom of this function you'll see event.waitUntil(promise);. Because of that, you're wrapping everything you do here in a promise, and when you resolve it will depend on what action the user takes.

The first thing you'll do is to close the notification regardless of what action the user takes. That's done with event.notification.close().

If the user clicked the button to feed Peggy, event.action should equal "feed." If the browser supports the action property, you can make a call to your feed endpoint, which will update the timer on the server. As soon as that endpoint is finished, you can resolve your promise. Remember, though, not all browsers support action, so have a backup plan for your app in case event.property returns undefined due to a lack of browser support.

If, however, the user clicked the button that says to wait to feed Peggy, you don't actually need to do anything. The notification will just close.

Your last check is whether or not the user clicked somewhere else on the notification. When that happens, you want to take the user to your page. So you can check if the page is running by looking at all of the clients the service worker has control of. If there some are running, you can just navigate those clients to the appropriate page. If the browser tab has been closed and there are no active clients, you'll want to open a new window with self.clients.openWindow.

This example includes a query string parameter on that route. This is just to show how you might pass data from the notification event into your page.

Note   You may remember that a couple of chapters ago you used messaging events to send information from the service worker back into your client. This is just another way to do so.

You aren't actively doing anything with that param, but you could take that data and update the UI accordingly. Maybe based on what gets passed in there, you could set the appropriate fade level of the image (or whatever else you might want to do in your future apps).

Once the user has landed on the page, you can resolve the promise, and you're all done!

Looking Ahead

Now that you're getting ever closer to catching up with native apps and features that were previously exclusive to native, the next chapter is going to shift focus back to another area that native apps have traditionally been ahead in: app loading performance.

As soon as you've digested push notifications, let's go make your app load super-fast!

App Shell Architecture and Loading Performance

One of the most important things you can do for your users is to give them the content they're looking for as soon as possible. When you launch a native app, you're usually presented with a splash screen, and then you can see *something* in the app within a second or two. On the Web, though, oftentimes we're stuck with a white screen for several seconds. Progressive web apps are here to help you change that with *app shell* architecture.

One of the interesting things about the app shell is that you've been using it all along and you've already implemented it. That's how sneaky fast it is!

What an App Shell Is

The app shell is just the bare minimum of UI you need to show the user something. That could be a navbar, a menu, some tabs, whatever. It's important that the user isn't staring at a blank white screen questioning if he or she really wants to be waiting for your app to finish loading. Then, once this skeleton of your app is visible, you can pull in your dynamic content.

The architecture part comes in when it's time to decide how you'll separate your static content (the app shell) from your dynamic content. App shell architecture is a natural fit for any front-end—heavy app that uses AJAX for dynamic content. Even when using front-end frameworks (which you'll see in a couple of chapters), you're able to utilize this architecture because those types of apps are already set up to separate the static content (the shell) from the dynamic content.

© Dennis Sheppard 2017
D. Sheppard, *Beginning Progressive Web App Development*, https://doi.org/10.1007/978-1-4842-3090-9_8

If, however, your app relies on the server sending full rendered pages and postbacks when responding to user input, you have a lot of architectural re-work to do.

Note   If you're unable to separate your static from dynamic content because you're exclusively using server-rendered pages, the app shell is probably not appropriate for your app.

To this point, our pirate app has already pretty much looked like a skeleton. There's really not that much content, and almost no styling, because we've focused on PWA concepts. So for this chapter, I've given iPatch a very corporate and grown-up makeover to illustrate what a proper app shell might look like, as you can see in Figures 8-1a and 8-1b.

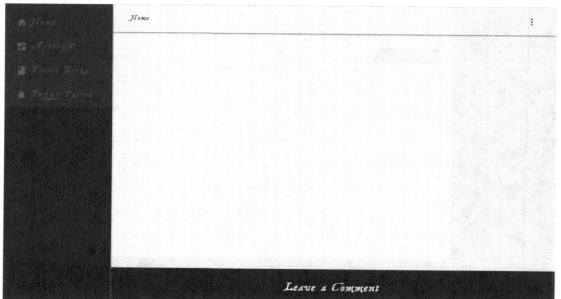

Figures 8-1a and 8-1b. *App shells for mobile and web*

Admittedly, this app doesn't have much more content than this anyway. But if you can get this much on the page in under a second (depending on connection, device, etc.), the user at least knows that, much like winter, more content is coming, as in Figures 8-2a and 8-2b.

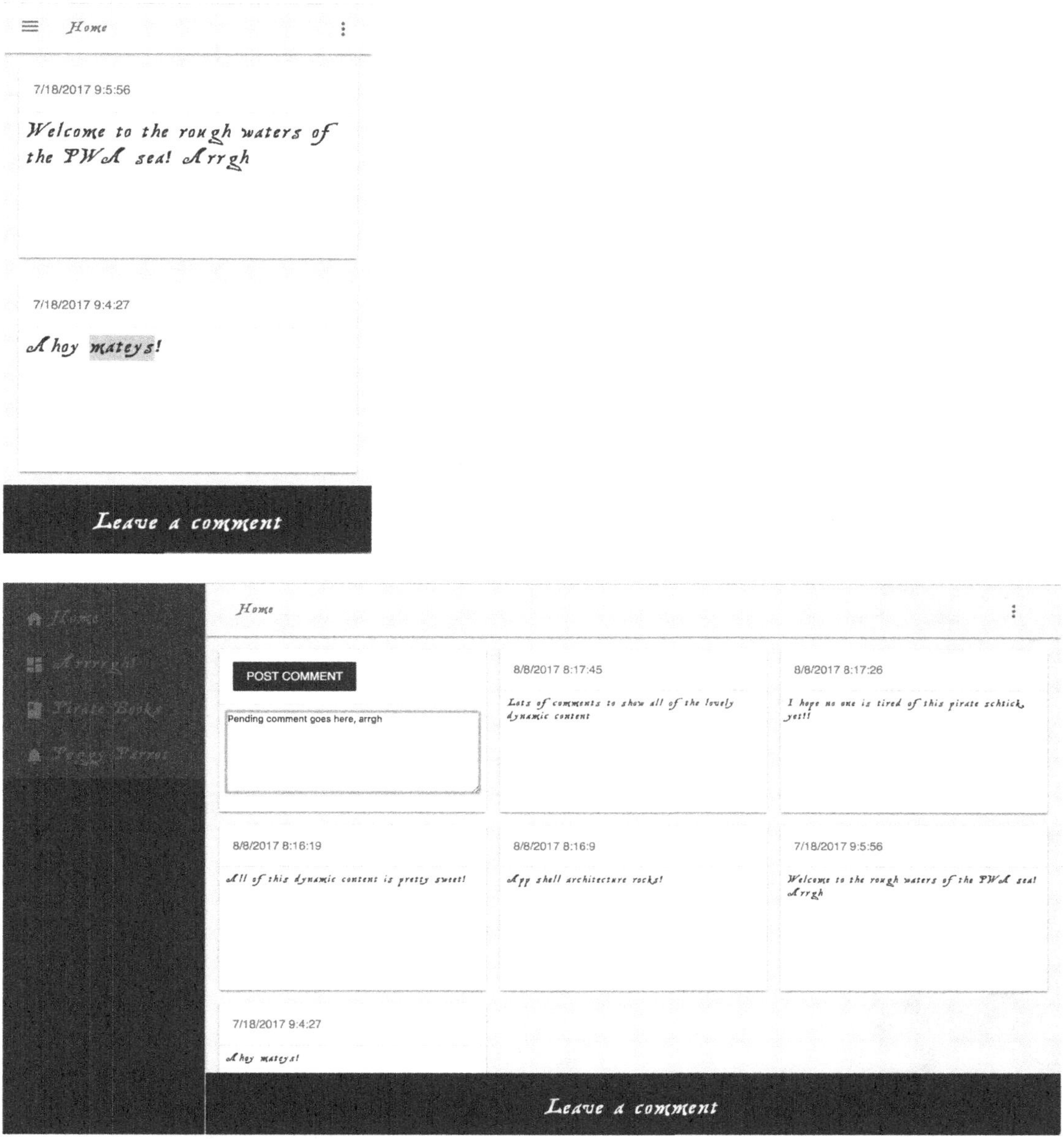

Figures 8-2a and 8-2b. *Once the dynamic content loads*

Caching the App Shell

The most important part of app shell architecture, though, is that you need to cache your app shell. Which makes a ton of sense, because your app shell doesn't change often. And if it does, you can easily clear the cache by updating your cache version when you deploy your UI changes.

In case you don't remember how to cache, you can use sw-precache if you are using a build system (or use it from the command line), or sw-toolbox, or you can just manually cache resources. You've actually been doing this all along with sw-toolbox, but in case you dropped into this chapter from the sky, let's take a look at how you're doing it.

In the service-worker.js file, you cache the app shell like so:

```
toolbox.router.get('/images/*', toolbox.cacheFirst, {
    cache: {
      name: CACHE_NAME,
      maxEntries: 20,
      maxAgeSeconds: 60 * 30
    }
});

  toolbox.router.get('/styles/*', toolbox.cacheFirst, {
    cache: {
      name: CACHE_NAME,
      maxEntries: 20,
      maxAgeSeconds: 60 * 60 * 24 * 7
    }
});

  toolbox.router.get('*.html', toolbox.cacheFirst, {
    cache: {
      name: CACHE_NAME,
      maxEntries: 20,
      maxAgeSeconds: 60 * 60 * 24 * 7
    }
});
```

I've named the CACHE_NAME to some string somewhere else, but name it whatever you'd like. Notice you're using the cacheFirst strategy for the app shell. That's kind of the whole point here is that you want the app shell as soon as you can possibly get it.

This method of caching will add to the cache whatever items the browser requests from your images or styles directories, as well as any HTML files. So once the user loads the app once, all subsequent visits to the site will use the cache instead.

Note   Remember, if you would like to *pre*-cache any files that user hasn't requested yet, you can do so with pre-cache. For example, you'll cache everything the user requests from index.html, and for the app shell, that's enough. But, once the user hits the index page, if you want the browser to cache other HTML files your app uses *before the user visits them*, you can do that with pre-cache.

At the top of the service worker, there are a few files you need access to in the service worker, namely the one that makes the toolbox object available:

```
importScripts('sw-toolbox.js', 'pirate-manager.js', 'localforage.min.js');
```

Once the service worker is registered (if you don't know how to do that, go back to Chapter 3!), the cache will be filled with all of the files necessary to build the app shell.

Now, to the extent you want to optimize rendering, you could even drop the styles directory from the cache and inline style the app shell for another notch of performance. You could fairly easily insert all styles into a <style> tag in the <head> of index.html.

Of course, there are obviously trade-offs in performance vs. maintainability as well as impacts to your caching strategy. If you inline styles you actually need elsewhere in your application, those styles won't be cached. Play around with various tweaks to inlining and caching to see what works for you. If you'd like to see any differences in rendering speed by moving around the styles, give it a shot and post a comment on the pirate comment board to let us know. As for this instance of iPatch, keep your separate CSS files for now.

Note   In another chapter you'll see if you can have the best of both worlds with HTTP/2 server push.

Being able to pull these resources from the cache (or even inlining them) instead of making a trip across the wires to a server can result in great performance benefits, as well as enable your app to show the application shell even while the user doesn't have an Internet connection.

Measuring App Shell Performance

In the case of the current pirate app iteration, caching the app shell took page load times on a laptop with a fast broadband connection from about 1.75 seconds on average without cached assets, down to about .75 with the cache, with some loads finishing in under .4 seconds! Again, this is not a very content-heavy site, but a 57% decrease in load time is still pretty fantastic.

Then, using WebPageTest with an emerging markets 3G connection on an Android device, subsequent page visits (using the cached app shell) resulted in about a 54% average reduction in the first page view. You can see the results at www.webpagetest. org/result/170809_0D_FK8/ and in Figure 8-3.

Performance Results (Median Run)

	Load Time	First Byte	Start Render	Speed Index	First Interactive (beta)	Document Complete			Fully Loaded			Cost
						Time	Requests	Bytes In	Time	Requests	Bytes In	
First View (Run 3)	6.350s	2.171s	2.294s	4335	2.390s	6.350s	12	171 KB	11.765s	19	288 KB	$---
Repeat View (Run 2)	2.886s	2.115s	2.215s	2483	2.842s	2.886s	6	39 KB	6.346s	12	156 KB	

Figure 8-3. *WebPageTest results with cached app shell*

Keep in mind that these numbers will vary depending on what measuring tool you're using, what device you're using, how heavy the network load is, what phase the moon is in, and if you're properly hydrated. Simply saying an app loads in under a second is meaningless without context.

For example, Lighthouse (discussed in Chapter 2) tends to show much higher load times than other tools like WebPageTest or browser plugins like "Page Load Time" and "Analyze Page Performance" because Lighthouse throttles both your network connection and your CPU to try to emulate a Nexus 5X. So if you can get your Lighthouse numbers down to something you're happy with, your desktop numbers should be superb!

Note   You can also simulate different connection speeds using DevTools under the *Network* tab. This will load your page as though your connection is limited to whichever option you choose.

Going Beyond the App Shell

If you've already pulled down the `chapter8` branch from `github.com/dennissheppard/pwa`, you may have noticed a couple of additional changes I haven't discussed. There are seemingly an infinite number of tips and tricks for performance to try to eke out another few milliseconds. While web apps are still fighting the performance perception wars against native apps, each blink of an eye can be important.

In Figure 8-4, let's compare what the Lighthouse performance section looks like if you run it with the code in the last chapter vs. the code in this chapter with the new app shell (and other performance tweaks I'll mention in a moment).

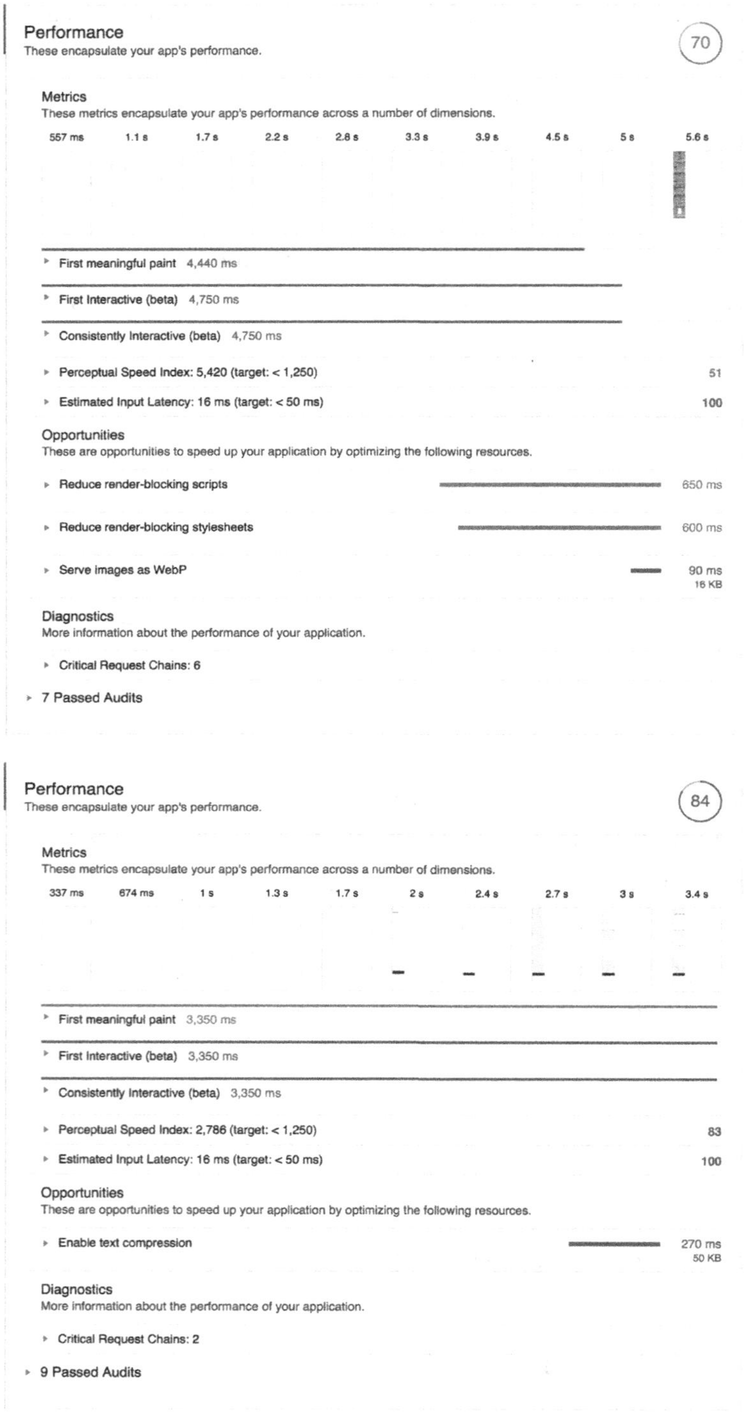

Performance   (70)
These encapsulate your app's performance.

Metrics
These metrics encapsulate your app's performance across a number of dimensions.

557 ms	1.1 s	1.7 s	2.2 s	2.8 s	3.3 s	3.9 s	4.5 s	5 s	5.6 s

» First meaningful paint 4,440 ms

» First Interactive (beta) 4,750 ms

» Consistently Interactive (beta) 4,750 ms

» Perceptual Speed Index: 5,420 (target: < 1,250)   51

» Estimated Input Latency: 16 ms (target: < 50 ms)   100

Opportunities
These are opportunities to speed up your application by optimizing the following resources.

» Reduce render-blocking scripts   650 ms

» Reduce render-blocking stylesheets   600 ms

» Serve images as WebP   90 ms
                                                             16 KB

Diagnostics
More information about the performance of your application.

» Critical Request Chains: 6

» 7 Passed Audits

Performance   (84)
These encapsulate your app's performance.

Metrics
These metrics encapsulate your app's performance across a number of dimensions.

337 ms	674 ms	1 s	1.3 s	1.7 s	2 s	2.4 s	2.7 s	3 s	3.4 s

» First meaningful paint 3,350 ms

» First Interactive (beta) 3,350 ms

» Consistently Interactive (beta) 3,350 ms

» Perceptual Speed Index: 2,786 (target: < 1,250)   83

» Estimated Input Latency: 16 ms (target: < 50 ms)   100

Opportunities
These are opportunities to speed up your application by optimizing the following resources.

» Enable text compression   270 ms
                                                             50 KB

Diagnostics
More information about the performance of your application.

» Critical Request Chains: 2

» 9 Passed Audits

Figure 8-4. *Lighthouse performance comparison*

147

You can see that not only did the pirate app get a UI and UX makeover, but it also got a pretty nice performance boost! Of course, going from a 70 to an 84 doesn't mean much without context. Notice that the time before the app was first interactive (that a user can actually do something on the page) was about a second and a half faster on the new site, and the Perceptual Speed Index (which measures how quickly content lands on the page) was almost 3 seconds faster.

So how did all this magic happen? Most of that magic is found right there in Lighthouse. Look at the first image under the *Opportunities* section. Lighthouse says that you have render blocking scripts and styles to take care of.

Render Blocking Scripts

A *render blocking script* is just what it sounds like. Once the browser has HTML markup, it begins to build the DOM by parsing the HTML. But while parsing the markup, the browser just goes in order. So that means if the HTML references a script, it stops the parsing to download and execute the script. As you can imagine, between fetching that new resource, executing it, then going back to parsing, all of this could significantly delay how fast the page loads.

Note   Stylesheets count as render blocking resources as well! If you're referencing stylesheets that aren't absolutely necessary to render your app shell, move them to the bottom of the HTML just before the `</body>` tag.

In order to fix this, you just need to move your scripts out of the *head* of your site and into the *body* so that the HTML isn't blocked. The *head* of the index.html file now just contains the manifest:

```
<head>
    <link rel="manifest" href="manifest.json">
</head>
```

Whereas before, the head contained a reference to each of your scripts and the CSS file:

```
<head>
    <script src="node_modules/localforage/dist/localforage.min.js"></script>
    <script src="pirate-manager.js"></script>
```

```
<script src="script.js"></script>
<link rel="stylesheet" type="text/css" href="styles/pirates.css"/>
<link rel="manifest" href="manifest.json">
<script src="companion.js" data-service-worker="service-worker.js"></script>
</head>
```

Each of those resources was delaying your page from rendering. Of course, if there is a script that is absolutely necessary to execute before you show your app shell, you can leave that in the *head*. But you should keep that script as small as possible, and consider inlining the script to keep the browser from having to fetch and download the file.

To inline a script, just put the contents of it between `<script></script>` tags. You're actually already doing this on a few of the pirate app pages, like `pirate_books.html`. Of course, in that case, none of that script is necessary to render the app shell, so you could (and probably should!) move that code to an external file and reference it near the bottom of the HTML.

Async and Defer

For modern browsers, there are a couple of additional options to keep your scripts from blocking the page rendering process.

The `async` keyword in a `script` tag will tell the browser to continue rendering the page while the resource is being downloaded, and will only pause parsing the HTML to execute that script. This is helpful for times when you want your script to execute as soon as possible, but don't need it to render your app shell. The drawback, however, is that async scripts aren't guaranteed to execute in any particular order. So if you have `library.js` and `scriptThatNeedsLibrary.js`, you can't use `async` without additional code to ensure the dependent script doesn't try to execute before the browser loads and executes script it depends on.

The `defer` keyword on a `script` tag tells the browser that the script can definitely wait for the HTML to render. The browser will still download the file as it is parsing HTML, but it won't execute the script until it's finished rendering. As a bonus, the browser's script execution stays true to the order in which you list the scripts. So scripts dependent on one another will execute in the order you would expect while using `defer`. Again, unless your app shell is absolutely dependent upon a script, this should be

your go-to. While it's support isn't completely universal (Opera doesn't support it), it's widely enough supported that you should probably always use defer. You get the best of both worlds by putting your scripts at the bottom of your HTML file while also using the defer keyword:

```
<!-- some HTML here →
<script defer src="https://code.getmdl.io/1.3.0/material.min.js"></script>
<script defer src="localforage.min.js"></script>
<script defer src="pirate-manager.js"></script>
<script defer src="script.js"></script>
<script defer src="companion.js" data-service-worker="service-worker.js">
</script>
</body>
```

You can compare the loading timeline of async and defer to the "regular process" in Figure 8-5.

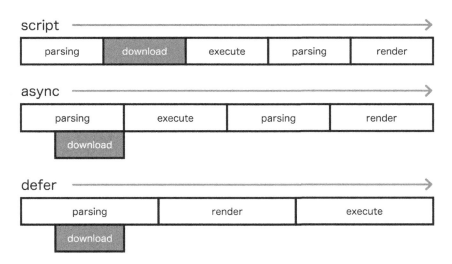

Figure 8-5. *How the browser handles regular script tags vs. the defer tag vs. the async tag*

Deferring Stylesheet Parsing and Execution

So this takes care of your scripts, but what about your stylesheets? The same principles apply here. Any CSS you don't need to render the app shell should be referenced at the bottom of the page. With stylesheets, however, we don't have the luxury of the defer or async keywords. So there are other... *hacks*, so to speak, we can use to defer the parsing and execution of stylesheets.

The link tag we use to reference stylesheets takes a media attribute that tells the browser to only parse that stylesheet if the provided media query is true. So if you give the media attribute a media query that is always going to be false, say the string "none" for example, the browser won't parse that stylesheet. That doesn't do you a lot of good if you do eventually need the stylesheet, so step two of this... *hack* is to include an onload event in the link tag that updates the media query:

```
<link rel="stylesheet" type="text/css" href="styles/pirates.css"
media="none"
        onload="if (media != 'all') media = 'all' "/>
```

This sets the media query to true, and the browser parses and executes the stylesheet once the onload event fires.

Of course, if you do that with all of your CSS, you'll notice the page first render on the screen with a flicker of unstyled content, which is probably not what you want. If you run the Chapter8-example-1_app_shell branch of the PWA repository, try adding the media property and onload events to the link tags and you'll see this happen. While this could boost your rendering time in some benchmarks, it's not very helpful to the user. So any CSS you need to properly render your app shell you could separate out into an app_shell.css file and include that in the head. Of course, if your app shell is dependent upon a CSS framework, that's much trickier because you typically wouldn't split apart the framework's CSS file to pull out just what you need for the app shell. In that case, you don't have much of a choice but to include the CSS file in the <head> tag.

Preloading JavaScript and CSS and Other Resources

There is a way to tell the browser that you'll need certain resources right away, before any of the rendering happens. This can be an important performance strategy because it can cut down on the number of steps the browser has to perform if the CSS the page needs is already downloaded and in place, for example. Or maybe you have a script that

is needed for early DOM manipulation or animations that should be in place before rendering starts. Because you request these so early in the page lifecycle, there's less of a chance that page rendering will be blocked.

You can preload these resources with the rel="preload" attribute. This tells the browser you need to preload that particular resource:

```
<link rel="preload" href="libs/styles/material-icons.css" as="style" />
<link rel="preload" href="libs/styles/material.blue_grey-indigo.min.css"
as="style" />
<link rel="preload" href="styles/pirates.css" as="style" />
```

Note that you've added preload to the link tag, and you've also included the as attribute, which tells the browser what kind of resource the file is. It also allows the browser to properly prioritize resource loading and match any future requests that might use that same resource.

This link, however, simply tells the browser to download the resource. To actually *use* the resource, you need to reference the files again using your regular link tags as well.

You can use this feature on several types of resources, including stylesheets, scripts, video, audio, fonts, images, and even fetches, and more.

If you include a MIME type on the resource, the browser can tell immediately if that resource is supported by the browser, and if not, the browser won't download a resource it can't use anyway:

```
<link rel="preload" href="libs/styles/material-icons.css" as="style"
type="text/css" />
<link rel="preload" href="videos/pirate-video.mp4" as="video" type="video/mp4" />
```

Note   Unfortunately you won't find a pirate video in the repo. That was just to show a non-CSS example.

Preload has good browser support and won't break older browsers, though if you try to preload a resource you're not actually using, Chrome will throw a warning in the DevTools console that you may have preloaded a resource unnecessarily. If you would like to preload resources you won't use until future page navigations, you can use the prefetch attribute instead of preload.

Telling the browser to prefetch resources doesn't guarantee they're downloaded right away. After all, you're not going to use them immediately. Instead, it's basically a heads up to the browser that you think they'll be needed in the future, and it's up to the browser to decide when to download them.

```
<link rel="prefetch" href="libs/styles/material-icons.css" />
<link rel="prefetch" href="libs/styles/material.blue_grey-indigo.min.css" />
<link rel="prefetch" href="styles/pirates.css" />
```

Notice that prefetch loses the as attribute of link.

Looking Ahead

Now that you've optimized a fair bit on the front end, it's time to shift focus to a server-side technology. In the next chapter I'll discuss HTTP/2 server push and how you might be able achieve the best of both inlining resources as well as caching them.

Exploring HTTP/2 and Server Push

We have a lot to be thankful for from HTTP. Wikipedia calls Hypertext Transfer Protocol the "foundation of data communication for the World Wide Web." Established way back in 1991, with version 1.1 coming onto the scene in 1999, HTTP has been around the block a few times. It has allowed us to communicate with others from every corner of the globe. It has created relationships and knowledge sharing and the ability to look at cute puppy pictures on a whim. And for all of these things and many more, we are grateful. But as is so common as time slips by, our beloved Hypertext Transfer Protocol has shown its age. As the Web has grown, bandwidth has increased, and users are demanding richer content, HTTP 1.1 (the version you're probably most familiar with) has shown some fundamental problems.

Chief among them are *head-of-line blocking* and lack of *header compression*. In this chapter, I'll briefly cover what those are and the trouble they've caused. But only as a backdrop to the solution we have before us: the successor to HTTP 1.1, which is HTTP/2. The bulk of this chapter will talk about what HTTP/2 is and how it's going to change your life as a developer and as a user of the Web. I'll cover how to implement HTTP/2 and one of the most important aspects of it with regards to PWAs and performance: *server push*. The history lesson won't be long, so if you're really itching to get to the implementation details, just remember what your good friend Billy Shakespeare said: *What's past is prologue.*

Head-of-Line Blocking

We teach our youngest children in school to form orderly queues and to wait their turns. HTTP 1.1 is really good at forcing requests to stay in line and to make each one wait its turn. This is why we have the render blocking issues discussed in the previous

© Dennis Sheppard 2017
D. Sheppard, *Beginning Progressive Web App Development*, https://doi.org/10.1007/978-1-4842-3090-9_9

chapter. Oftentimes, we put a lot of demands on HTTP; lots of requests to fill the rich media needs our sites and apps require. But HTTP 1.1 is only able to handle a handful of requests before it blocks subsequent requests, so that they have to wait for whatever resource is at the head of the line.

Let's take a look at our beloved pirate app and the requests it makes via HTTP 1.1 in Figure 9-1.

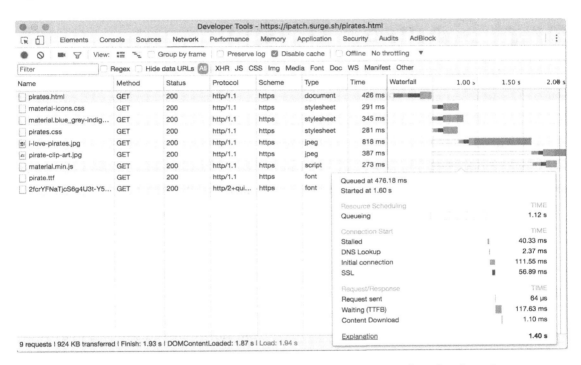

Figure 9-1. *HTTP 1.1 requests forming an orderly queue after the first three requests*

Here you see that HTTP 1.1 is able to make a few requests in parallel. Eventually, though, you can see the requests start to queue up. You can even see how long a resource has to wait its turn before the request is fulfilled. They're so well behaved and patient!

But when you do the same thing using HTTP/2 (with multiple useless scripts added in just to show what HTTP/2 is capable of), you can see in Figure 9-2 that the requests are all kicked off at the same time.

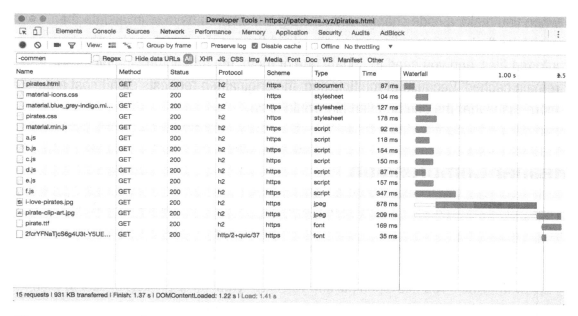

Figure 9-2. *HTTP/2 requests kick off as soon as the browser reaches them in the HTML, which usually results in better load times*

This is because HTTP/2 uses a single, bidirectional stream between client and server, rather than the multiple connection architecture HTTP 1.1 uses because it's only able to deliver one request at a time. Multiple requests are made via this single connection. This is called *multiplexing.* All of this magic allows requests to happen at the same time inside of that one request so that any particular request isn't blocked by others closer to the head of the line.

Note   Multiplexing in and of itself isn't new. In all of your additional research, you may run across a technology called SPDY. This technology modified existing requests via HTTP 1.1 and contained a few of the improvements that HTTP/2 has. Multiplexing was one of those. SPDY is now deprecated in favor of HTTP/2.

Because of multiplexing, requests using HTTP/2 are much more efficient. As a result, concatenating and bundling files, one of the big performance improvements often utilized with HTTP 1.1, is actually an anti-pattern with HTTP/2. Instead of a giant bundled or concatenated file that might take a couple of seconds to download, if code is split up into smaller packages, you're able to utilize the cache more efficiently while not having additional requests cost anything. For example,

157

when you make a code change with one big bundle, you have to invalidate the cache for that entire bundle and re-download the asset. If that bundle is broken into ten files, and you need to update one of them, the remaining nine files can remain cached. Because of multiplexing, the original ten requests didn't cost any more than what the one bundled file would have.

Header Compression

If this was 30 years ago and you were going to mail a letter, there was a bunch of additional information on the outside of that letter that let the mail carriers know where it should go, how it should get there, and where to send it back in case something unforeseen happened along the way.

Now imagine if you had a pen pal and you each wrote these packets of data to each other, back and forth, and the amount of data on the exterior of each of those packets kept adding up. Your hand would get tired from writing out the full addresses, and then your pen pal would have to do the same. You might shudder to think that if you became famous you would have had bags and bags of fan mail! So many requests that require an equal number of responses.

It would've been more efficient if there was a way to reduce the amount of data that the postal service required to send your actual data.

Much like the postal service in the days of yore, HTTP headers contain information about data that's passing across the wires, whether that data is a request to a server or a response to a client. And sure, individually each header doesn't require a lot of bandwidth; just a few bytes here and there. But if your site has dozens of requests and then dozens of responses (and remember that as good PWA devs, we're also conscious of low-bandwidth users!), those bytes really add up. Additionally, headers aren't very efficient and oftentimes header data that isn't needed for each request is attached to all requests anyway. So there is lots of room for improvement with header compression, which would essentially shrink the amount of bandwidth required to transmit header data.

Even though HTTP 1.1 didn't supply a way to reduce all of this extra data, SPDY did. Unfortunately, that mechanism for header compression had security vulnerabilities that led to the ability for hackers to hijack browser sessions, even for sites served over a secure HTTPS connection. This was known as a *CRIME* attack, or "Compression Ratio Info-leak Made Easy."

So that wasn't good.

Header compression, as an idea, is good, though. And that's why HTTP/2 uses a compression algorithm called *HPACK* that not only compresses headers, but also reduces redundant header data. The details of *HPACK* are out of scope of what I'll cover here, but rest assured those security flaws are all patched up.

Introducing HTTP/2

Now that you know some of the problems that HTTP/2 solves, and how it does it, let's take a step back and talk about what HTTP/2 actually is.

HTTP/2 is the first upgrade to HTTP since 1999. The primary goal of HTTP/2 is to improve website performance and security. I talked about some of the performance benefits, but on the security side, if you want that sweet performance boost, browsers require TLS connections in order to use HTTP/2.

So now with HTTP/2, we have better performance with multiplexing, header compression, and server push (more on that in a moment), and better security with HTTPS requirements. HTTP/2 does all of this while maintaining backwards compatibility with HTTP 1.1. Browser support for HTTP/2 is excellent, but if you're stuck supporting old browsers, don't sweat it. You're in good shape.

By now you're probably jumping out of your seat with excitement. Enough of all this talk; let's actually *use* HTTP/2!

Implementing HTTP/2 in Node.js

If you want to run a local dev server, you can actually implement an extremely rudimentary one with HTTP/2 pretty easily. If you don't have the *PWA Book* project, go ahead and pull down the `Chapter9-example-1_http2` branch. The completed code from this chapter will be in `server.js`, so if you want to follow along, change the name of that file and follow along with us. It'll be fun!

First, let's install your dependencies by running

```
npm install --save spdy express mz
```

The `spdy` npm package will allow you to create an HTTP/2 server with a SPDY fallback. You've used *Express* before; you'll use that to serve your files. And finally `mz` will allow you to use some ES6 syntax like promises.

Now, create a new directory in the PWA Book directory. Call it http2-server. Create a new JavaScript file in there and call it server.js or whatever you'd like. There are about a dozen and a half lines of code that you need to create your server:

```
const port = 8081;
const express = require('express');
const spdy = require('spdy');
const fs = require('mz/fs');

const app = express();

const cert = {
            key: fs.readFileSync('./localhost.key'),
            cert: fs.readFileSync('./localhost.cert')
          };

app.use(express.static('../'));

app.get('*', (req, res) => {
  res.status(200);
});

spdy.createServer(cert, app)
    .listen(port, console.log('Listening on port: ' + port));
```

This is all the code you need to serve the pirate app on HTTP/2. First, you define your port and bring in your dependencies. You reference Express, and then because HTTP/2 requires SSL, you need to give the server a key and cert file. If you were running this in prod, you would need to procure an actual cert. But for local testing, you can generate one yourself. To do so, in your terminal, navigate to the http2-server directory and run the following command:

```
openssl req  -nodes -new -x509  -keyout localhost.key -out localhost.cert
```

The result of this will be a series of questions that will be used to generate your key and cert files. Once that's done, you have your HTTPS site, but it won't be trusted by the browser. Browsers don't like self-signed certificates. You'll see the repercussions of that in a moment, but for our purposes, this will work just fine.

After you assign your cert, tell Express to serve up the directory with all of your front-end files in it. Next, define a route for any GET requests, returning a 200 if the request is successful. Feel free to put code in there to handle any bad requests, but you won't be using this code for long, so don't sweat it if you don't feel like it.

Finally, you ask your spdy package to go ahead and create the web server using your cert and app objects. That's it. You have a working HTTP/2 server.

Head back to your terminal and if you're still in the `http2-server` directory, you can run

```
node server.js
```

Your server is now running and you can navigate to `https://localhost:8081`. As in Figure 9-3, you will be greeted rather rudely by your browser.

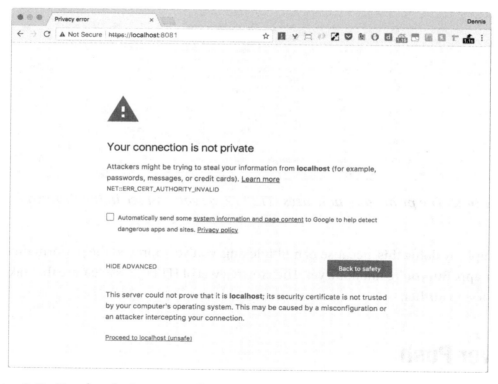

Figure 9-3. *Don't take it personally. Browsers don't trust any self-signed certs. They aren't secure!*

You created the certificate, so you can safely click the Advanced link (or whatever your browser shows) and choose to proceed. Again, in production, you'll want a cert signed by a Certificate Authority.

Once you proceed, you should see the pirate app! Maybe that's a little anti-climactic. After all, you've seen this trifling little app for like a million chapters at this point. But in this case, it's not about what the app shows. Pull up DevTools and refresh the page. Go to the *Network* tab.

If you don't see the *Protocol* column, right-click on one of the column headers and add it. In Figure 9-4 you will see *h2* almost all the way down, indicating that your files were served from HTTP/2. The exception here is your API call, because the API server isn't using HTTP/2.

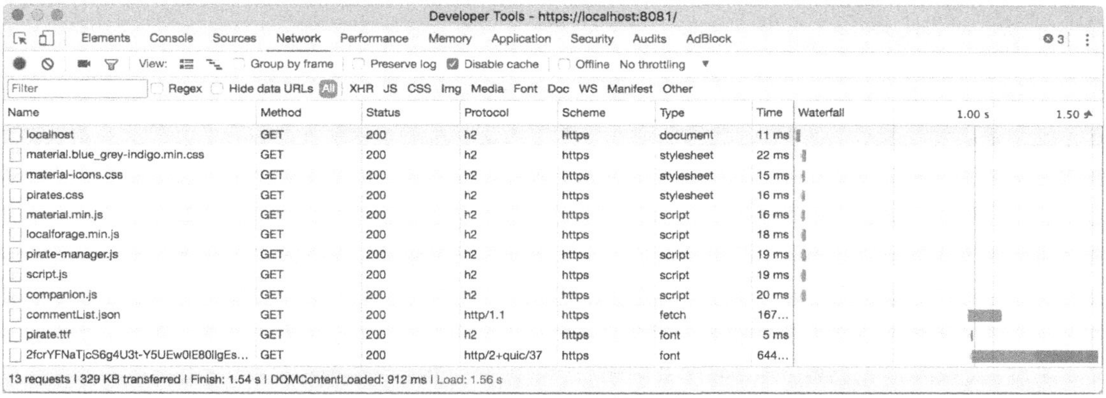
Developer Tools - https://localhost:8081/
Elements Console Sources Network Performance Memory Application Security Audits AdBlock
View: Group by frame Preserve log Disable cache Offline No throttling
Filter Regex Hide data URLs All XHR JS CSS Img Media Font Doc WS Manifest Other
Name Method Status Protocol Scheme Type Time Waterfall 1.00 s 1.50
localhost GET 200 h2 https document 11 ms
material.blue_grey-indigo.min.css GET 200 h2 https stylesheet 22 ms
material-icons.css GET 200 h2 https stylesheet 15 ms
pirates.css GET 200 h2 https stylesheet 16 ms
material.min.js GET 200 h2 https script 16 ms
localforage.min.js GET 200 h2 https script 18 ms
pirate-manager.js GET 200 h2 https script 19 ms
script.js GET 200 h2 https script 19 ms
companion.js GET 200 h2 https script 20 ms
commentList.json GET 200 http/1.1 https fetch 167...
pirate.ttf GET 200 h2 https font 5 ms
2fcrYFNaTjcS6g4U3t-Y5UEw0lE80IlgEs... GET 200 http/2+quic/37 https font 644...
13 requests | 329 KB transferred | Finish: 1.54 s | DOMContentLoaded: 912 ms | Load: 1.56 s

Figure 9-4. *The pirate app now uses HTTP/2, as you can see in the Protocol column.*

Simply by doing this, because of multiplexing, you've improved the performance of your app. But you're not done yet. The crown jewel of HTTP/2 is a feature that takes things a step further.

Server Push

In the normal course of your request-response lifecycle, the client asks for an index page and the server responds. The client parses that page and sees that there are additional resources it needs, like CSS files or JavaScript or whatever. The client requests them and the server responds. Request-response, request-response, and on and on it goes, as you can see in Figure 9-5.

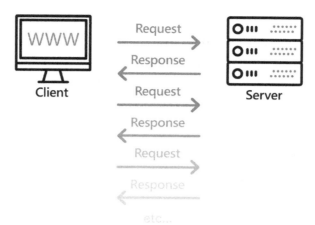

Figure 9-5. *Normal request-response pattern between a client and server*

What if, though, you knew ahead of time that the client was going to request certain resources? Couldn't you push those resources to the client at the same time that you delivered the original index file? That would save multiple request-response cycles and *even further improve performance.* You'd be a hero! If only there was a way...

Introducing HTTP/2 *server push*! You can configure your server to send certain files along with routes that you specify, thereby reducing as many round trips to the server as files you push to the client. Compare Figure 9-5 with Figure 9-6.

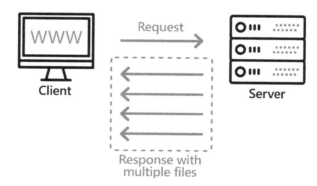

Figure 9-6. *Server push pattern, where the server sends certain resources along with the initial request*

There are, of course, drawbacks. If you push files to the client that were already cached, that's a waste of bandwidth and could actually slow down your app. Thus, like with most of the features I've talked about that deal with performance, you should test your app and experiment with these technologies to see what works best for your particular situation.

For the pirate app, try pushing your main CSS file and your `pirate-manager.js` file. You, of course, could push more than this, but this is for illustrative purposes, plus remember the caveat about pushing resources vs. caching them. Let's take a look at how you can implement server push with your HTTP/2 `Express.js` server:

```
const port = 8081;
const express = require('express');
const spdy = require('spdy');
const fs = require('mz/fs');

const app = express();

const cert = {
            key: fs.readFileSync('./localhost.key'),
            cert: fs.readFileSync('./localhost.cert')
        };

const index = fs.readFileSync('../index.html');
const css = fs.readFileSync('../styles/pirates.css');
const pirateManager = fs.readFileSync('../scripts/pirate-manager.js');

app.use(express.static('../'));

app.get('/home', (req, res) => {

    let cssResource = {
      path: '/styles/pirates.css',
      contentType: 'text/css',
      file: css
    };

    let pirateManagerResource = {
      path: '/scripts/pirate-manager.js',
      contentType: 'application/javascript',
      file: pirateManager
    };
```

```
    pushResource(res, cssResource);
    pushResource(res, pirateManagerResource);

    res.writeHead(200);
    res.end(index);
});

function pushResource(res, resource) {
  let stream = res.push(resource.path, {
      req: {'accept': '**/*'},
      res: {'content-type': resource.contentType}
    });

    stream.on('error', err => {
      console.log(err);
    });

    stream.end(resource.file);
}

spdy.createServer(cert, app)
    .listen(port, console.log('Listening on port: ' + port));
```

This is quite a bit more code than before, but you are doing quite amazing things with it! Let's break it down.

Everything up top all the way down past your cert is the same. Right after that, you need to grab the files that you want to push. In your case, that'll be index.html, pirate.css, and pirate-manager.js. The server file is currently nested in your http2-server directory, so you have to move up a level to access those files. So far so good.

Your setup to use the express static file server is the same as before. Then you set up a route just like before, but in this case you're changing your route a little. It's likely that you wouldn't want to push the same resources to every part of your app. So here you've set up a new route to your landing page, called *home*. You could set up a route to Peggy's page and call it *peggy*, or a route to the books page and call it *books*. In each of those cases, though, it's extremely likely that you would have already cached all of your resources, so pushing those same ones to them might not make sense. Your mileage may vary here.

165

Inside of the route, you're setting up a couple of resource objects that contain information about each resource, including their path, content type, and a reference to the files you created further up. Last, you call the pushResource function, passing in a reference to your response object and the resource object, respond to the request with a 200, and close the response by sending your index.html file.

Note   The path here is different than the reference to the file because at this point you're in the context of the request, so there's no need to move up a directory to access the file.

Let's now peek inside the pushResource function. response.push is the key here because it is telling the response to push the file found at that path. You pass in header information, check for errors, and close up the stream that is pushing the file.

You can run this server from the http2-server directory just like you did the last version of your HTTP/2 server:

```
node server.js
```

Load up the site at https://localhost:8081/home. If you didn't already have DevTools up, bring them up, go to the *Navigation* tab and refresh the page. Look at the *Initiator* column in Figure 9-7 (right-click on the columns and add it if you don't already see it).

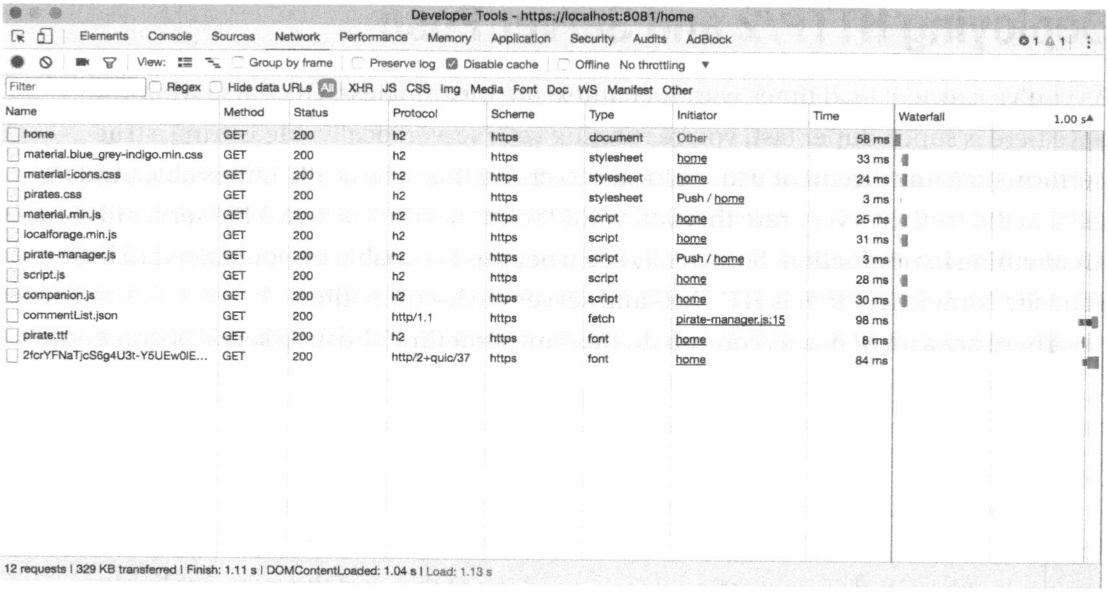

Figure 9-7. *The Initiator column tells what resources were pushed to the client*

You're actively pushing resources to the client! You can hover over the little slice of the bar chart for either resource that was pushed and see the breakdown of why it took so long, like in Figure 9-8. Three whole milliseconds is just ridiculous!

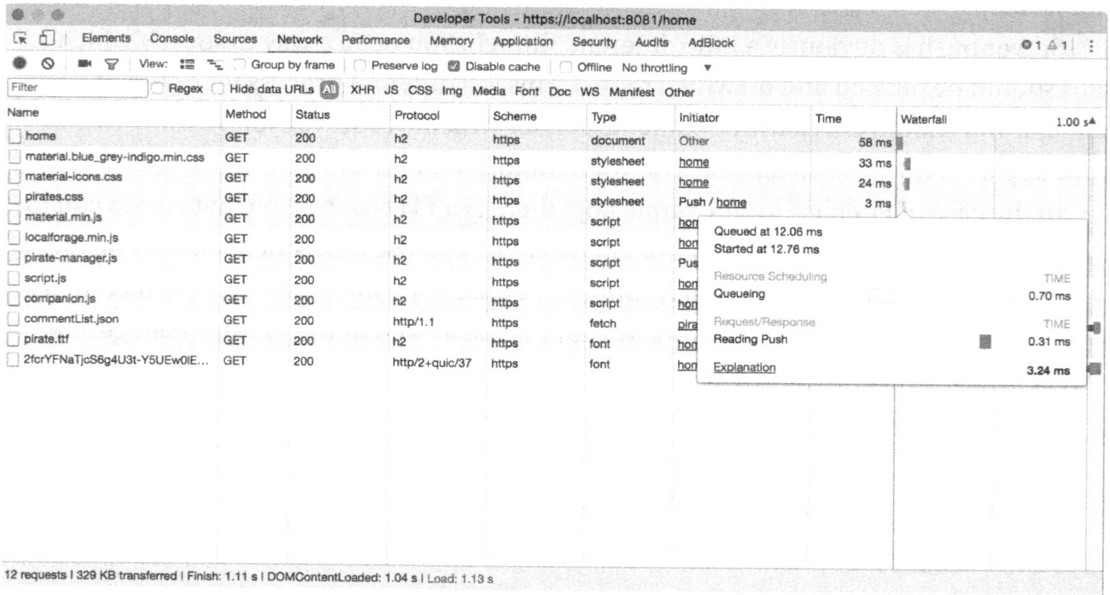

Figure 9-8. *The breakdown of a pushed resource*

Deploying HTTP/2 and Server Push

As you've learned, load times without context are meaningless. Of course what you have here is super-duper fast; you're running your server locally. Measuring a true performance improvement using a local server like this is basically impossible. And to tell you the truth, it's very rare that you would want to write your own file server like this for anything in production. So to really see what this is capable of, you'll need to host your site somewhere that is HTTP/2- and server push-compatible.

There are a lot of places you can do this, but sometimes hosting services don't make it obvious whether they support these features. Google Cloud Platform does, but it's overkill for what you need. Azure supports HTTP/2, but not server push. Heroku doesn't support either one.

A nice sweet spot for your needs is Firebase. It will allow easy deployment and supports HTTP/2 with server push. I won't walk through the steps to set up a Firebase project because its documentation does a good job of that and the steps are liable to change.

You might be wondering, though, how you actually implement HTTP/2 and server push if you're not writing the server yourself. The good news is that if your hosting provider supports HTTP/2, it will be enabled by default. And that in and of itself should provide you some performance improvements over HTTP 1.1. Oh, multiplexing, we're not worthy!

Server push is obviously a little different, though. You need a way to specify which files should be pushed and on which routes. This is a different process for different servers. You should check the documentation for whichever server you're using to host your app as to how you specify files for routes and server push.

In the case of Firebase for the pirate app, there is a `firebase.json` that allows you to include additional header information. In this case, you use a *Link* header. *Link* headers tell the client to look for additional resources. In the deployment here, you've included a *Link* header that as a value takes your `script.js` file as well as the `pirate-manager.js` and the `pirates.css` resources:

```
"headers": [
    {
      "source": "/",
      "headers": [
        {
```

```
        "key": "Link",
        "value": "<scripts/script.js>;rel=preload;as=script,
                  <scripts/pirate-manager.js>;rel=preload;as=script,
                  <styles/pirates.css>;rel=preload;as=style"
      }
    ]
  }
]
```

You're saying here that any route originating from your home directory, you should push these resources. The `rel=preload` and `as=` syntax might even look familiar. This is technically not the original intended purpose of those properties, which were intended for the browser to download those resources immediately. But lots of servers use this syntax now for server push. It's what you have for now, and it works as you can see in Figure 9-9.

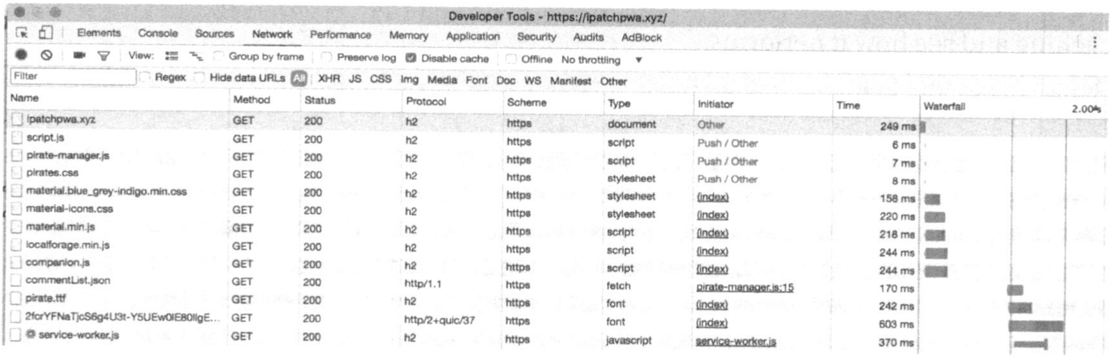

Figure 9-9. *Server push when your app is deployed to Firebase*

Measuring the Impact of HTTP/2 and Server Push

To see any performance difference, you should deploy the app to an HTTP 1.1 provider as well as an HTTP/2 provider. There might be times when HTTP 1.1 wins, particularly if you're more aggressive with your caching strategy.

This pirate app now lives in two places: `https://ipatch.surge.sh`, which is an HTTP 1.1 hosting service, and `https://ipatchpwa.xyz`, which is the Firebase deployment using server push. Figure 9-10 compares these two directly.

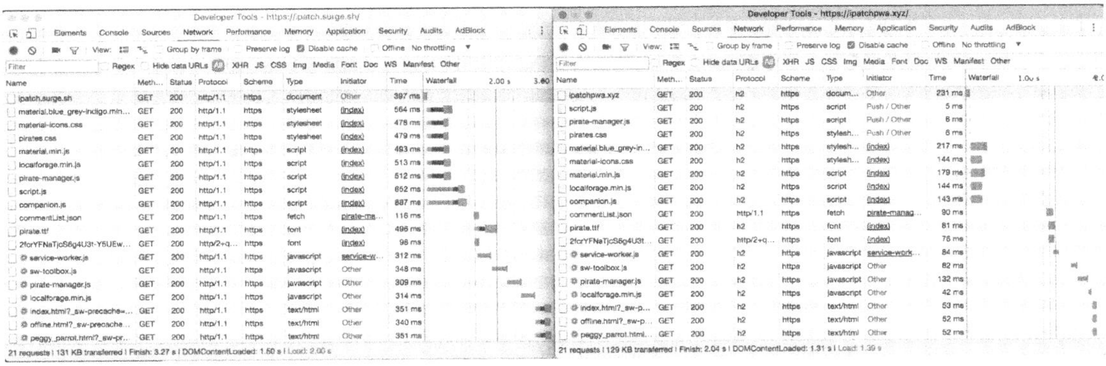

Figure 9-10. *Comparing HTTP 1.1 and HTTP/2 with server push*

If you haven't read it before, you should read it now. Measuring page load speed without context is meaningless. There are just too many variables, particularly when using a mobile connection and comparing across different servers, etc.

So you should try it out for yourself to see which one performs better and feels better. Try with and without server push. Check out the second page visit in Figure 9-11 with caching and see how it performs.

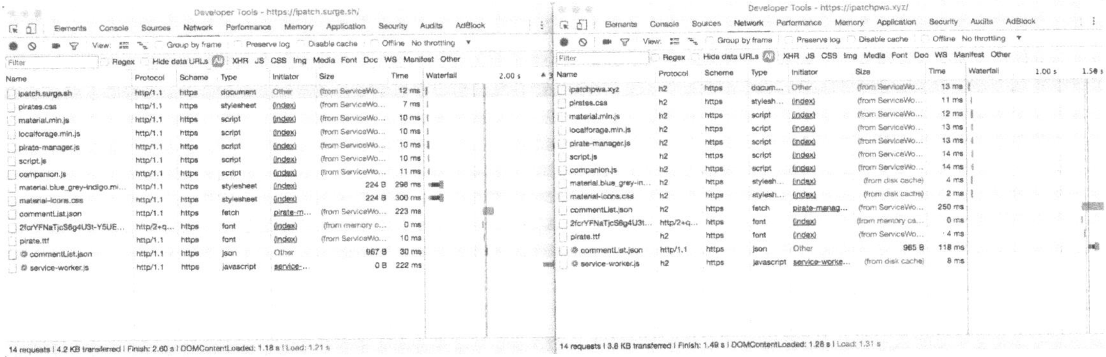

Figure 9-11. *Comparing the repeat page visit of HTTP 1.1 and HTTP/2 with server push and cached files*

On repeat visits, you're mostly using the service worker cache anyway, so there's hardly any visible difference between the two, and the load times are definitely within any margin of error due to whatever network hiccups or randomness you might experience.

However, the biggest difference here is one you can't see. Using DevTools doesn't allow you to see that the server is still pushing files and taking up bandwidth. That's

because pushed files reside in a server push cache, which is the last cache the browser checks for files. If the browser finds files that are still eligible in the service worker cache first, it will use those instead of the pushed ones. That means that the browser could actually use older (but unexpired) assets sitting in the service worker cache rather than newer assets that the server pushes.

These are trade-offs you have to consider when choosing whether to use server push. In the pirate app example, you get a noticeable performance improvement on first load when you use HTTP/2, but less so with server push. On subsequent page loads, because you're making heavy use of the cache, there isn't a significant performance boost from HTTP/2 over HTTP 1.1 on a broadband connection. What about over 3G, though? Check out Figure 9-12; to the Lighthouse!

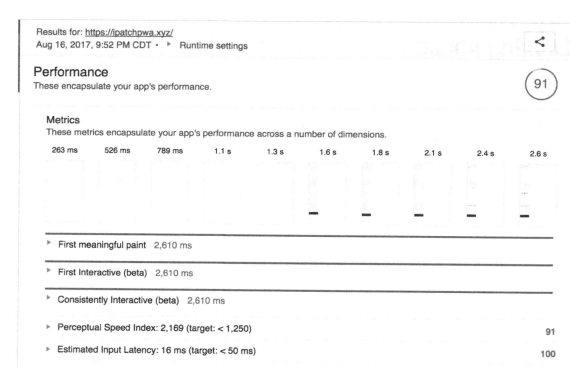

Figure 9-12. *Lighthouse results with HTTP/2 and server push*

The Firebase-deployed HTTP/2 with server push app is now rocking a very robust performance score of 91! Obviously if we ran this a few more times, that score could fluctuate up or down. But it is the highest we've seen so far, so let's take it and run! For this app, it looks like HTTP/2 with server push is the way to go.

Note   Of course, your app here is quite trivial, and there is a lot more to think about regarding your app's infrastructure and performance considerations. For a deeper look at HTTP/2 and various points I didn't cover here, check out Jack Archibald's blog post: `https://jakearchibald.com/2017/h2-push-tougher-than-i-thought/`.

Looking Ahead

Now it's time to really apply your PWA knowledge. With the conclusion of this chapter, the theory portion of your PWA education is complete. You've learned about service workers, caching, background syncing, app manifests, notifications, app shells, push notifications, and HTTP/2 server push. And while you've applied all of that theory to the frivolous little pirate app, it might really help these concepts to sink in if you apply some of them to an existing web app that's just begging to be PWA-ized. That's where you're headed next. Say goodbye to our pirate friends! For now...

PART III

Putting the Features to Use

Turning a Real App into a PWA

This is the moment you've been training for. Everything you've learned in the previous chapters has prepared you for this: your first chance to take an actual application and turn it into a PWA. None of that pirate stuff. This is the real deal. Kind of. Mostly. You'll be taking a fantastic open source app from GitHub that's in need of a little PWA love. First, you'll check out the app's Lighthouse scores for PWA and Performance. That'll give you an idea of where to start. You'll try to get as close to a perfect Lighthouse score as you can, but the main focus will be on making all sorts of PWA enhancements. You'll be adding a service worker (of course), you'll use pre-cache for the app shell, runtime caching to make the app work offline, an app manifest for adding an icon to the home screen (among other benefits), you'll implement server push, and any other suggestions Lighthouse has for you so you can crank up those PWA and Performance scores. Basically, you're taking the knowledge you've learned throughout this book (and maybe some things I haven't covered yet), and applying it to an existing, open source application. By the end of this chapter, you'll have a real live Progressive Web App!

The Movies Finder App

There are hundreds of thousands of open-source JavaScript projects on GitHub. After scouring that list for an inordinate amount of time for the perfect app to transform into a PWA, Mohammed Lazhari's `Movies Finder` app (`https://github.com/Lazhari/Movies-Finder`) appeared like an oasis in a desert.

You can see the current production version of the app at `https://movies-finder.firebaseapp.com/` and the version that contains our updates lives here: `https://github.com/dennissheppard/Movies-Finder`.

© Dennis Sheppard 2017
D. Sheppard, *Beginning Progressive Web App Development*, https://doi.org/10.1007/978-1-4842-3090-9_10

It's an Angular application built off of the Angular CLI. If you don't know Angular, **don't panic**. Nothing you've learned in this book is framework dependent, so this won't be any different. I'll stop to point out any places that you might need to tweak depending on your particular app's setup. I'll also stop to cover any Angular-specific concepts you need to make this app a PWA. It's likely, though, that you won't even have to dive deeply into the code, and you certainly won't be writing any Angular code.

Note   This is not to say you shouldn't fork either repo and experiment on your own. As you'll see, to really unlock the potential of this app, it's likely that you would need to make some functional and structural changes. Those types of changes, however, are simply out of scope for what you're trying to learn.

Let's start with is a brief description of the app. Movies Finder is an app that shows the most popular movies out right now and allows users to search for movies and view them by category. The movie data is from The Movie Database (`tmdb.org`), which provides an open API.

It's already mobile friendly, as you can see in Figure 10-1, so thankfully you won't need to do any visual makeovers.

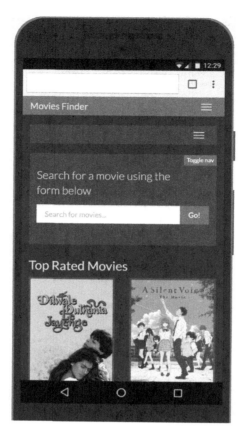

Figure 10-1. *Movies Finder on mobile*

There's no service worker and no caching, though. Because this is an image-heavy app, that's a lot of data being passed across the wires, and a big opportunity for caching.

The Angular production build process bundles and minifies the files, which is going to save some bytes. But the main bundle weighs in at 548KB, while a few other library files tack on another 40KB or so. Looking at Figure 10-2, you can see that the total first load is going to cost just under 2MB. That's a pretty hefty load, and unfortunately there's not a whole lot you can do to change it. It will just add to the challenge.

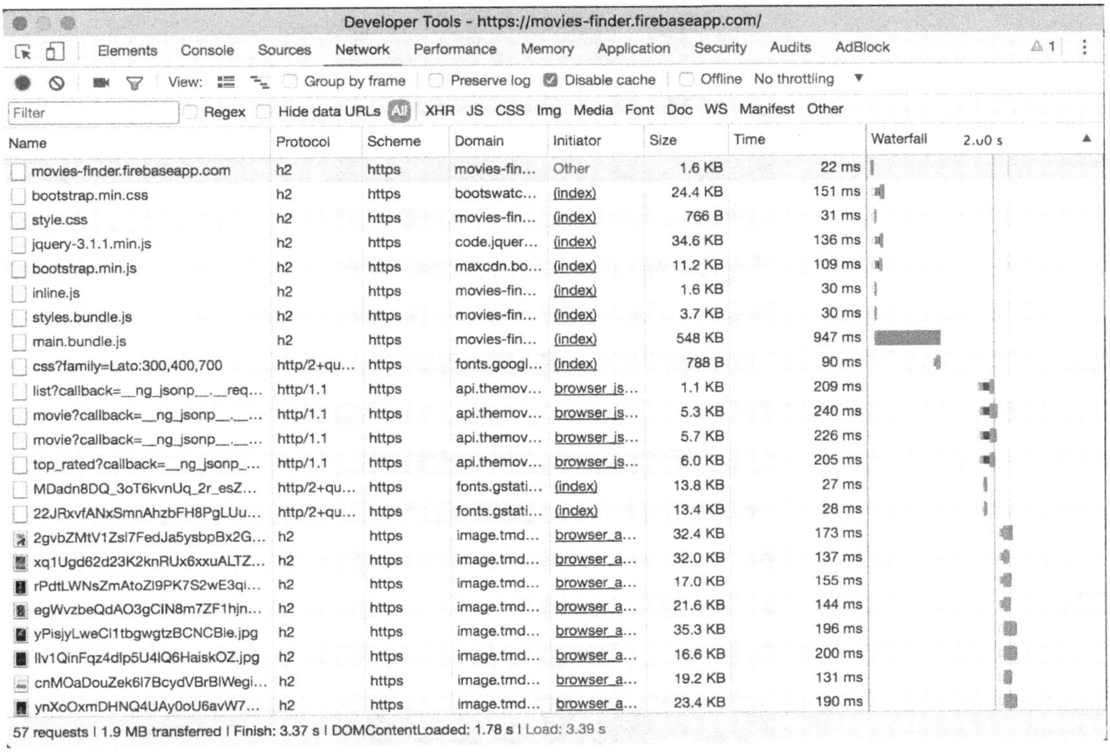

Figure 10-2. *The first page load of Movies Finder*

Because so many images are pulled down on that first load, performance times are going to be tough to improve. Repeat visits should fly, in comparison, once you put caching in place. But that first load is probably going to make Lighthouse very unhappy. The good news is that the app is hosted on Firebase so HTTP/2 is already in place, and it looks like those images are all getting kicked off simultaneously.

Speaking of Lighthouse, let's see the baseline (Figure 10-3).

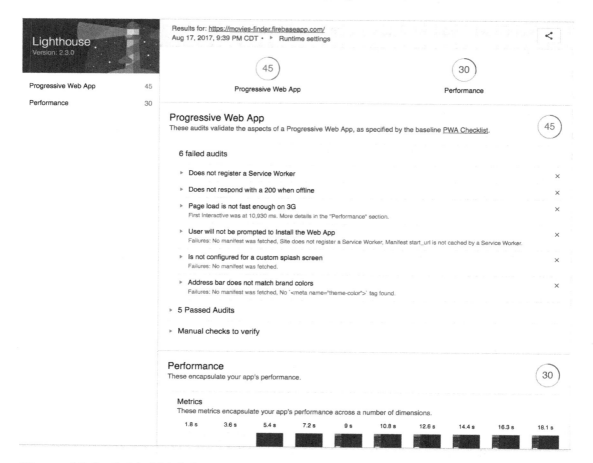

Figure 10-3. *Initial Lighthouse scores of Movies Finder*

Considering there's almost no PWA features in place here, a 45 for PWA and 30 for performance really isn't bad. It looks like the first meaningful paint arrived around the 9s mark. You'll make your target 5s, but again because the first load is so image heavy, that's going to be a challenge. Repeat visits, however, should be able to get into the 2s-3s range for mobile on 3G.

The Plan to Make a PWA

There's definitely some work to do here, but all in all you have a solid foundation to build on. This app is using a modern framework, it's already using HTTP/2, and the build process already bundles and minifies, and also should make it easy to add in sw-precache. There's already an app shell in place because the UI is separated from the logic; you just need to cache it. So that will be your first order of business. Once you set up sw-precache, you'll throw in runtime caching with sw-toolbox and make sure all of those images are in place for subsequent visits.

After those are in place, you'll check up on the Lighthouse scores and see where you're at. Then you should move on to the app manifest. That will be pretty straightforward and will improve the PWA score a healthy amount.

Next, you'll see if server push can cut a few ms off the load times for the main JavaScript bundle and see if there's anything else you can push, too. The app is already using a CDN for Bootstrap, but you may need to tweak that some if it's causing any problems.

Note   A CDN is a content delivery network. In short, a CDN is able to deliver content to users fast because the resources are distributed on a network, resulting in files being physically close to the user. Typically you'd want to use a CDN, but part of optimizing for performance is in experimenting to see what works.

You want the app to have a lot of offline-first capability, but there's a lot of data here, and it's not practical for the entire app to have offline availability. But the app should at least return a 200 and show *something* with no Internet connection.

That will cover almost every PWA and performance feature I've covered. Finally, depending on where the scores are after that, you'll see what other suggestions Lighthouse has for you to try to get closer and closer to PWA perfection. But don't stop there if you want to keep going! Once you've reached the PWA pinnacle of perfection with your Lighthouse score, there's still more to do. So there will be an exercise for you at the end of this chapter that takes the offline functionality a step further, if you're up to the challenge. Sound good? This is going to be fun!

> **Note**   What we're about to undertake, we're undertaking as a team. This app wasn't transformed in advance, so whatever scores we come out with, we're in this together. It's possible we'll fall short of some goals, but regardless of our load times and scores, we'll have a proper PWA at the end.

Getting the Code and Running It

The first thing you need to do is pull down the code for the app. As a reminder, there's a fork of the app available at https://github.com/dennissheppard/Movies-Finder. You're using a fork instead of the original repo because you'll be creating branches each step of the way, and I've upgraded this version of the app to use the latest version of Angular and the CLI (as of September, 2017, anyway). That's all been done for you. To get started, all you need to do is run the following in your terminal in whatever directory you want the app to live in:

```
git clone https://github.com/dennissheppard/Movies-Finder.git
cd Movies-Finder
npm install
```

Normally in an Angular app, you would now be able to run ng serve to run the application on port 4200 by default. However, ng serve bundles the app's assets and runs the app in memory. While this is fine for development of the app, you need to be able to set up caching for resources that you'll ultimately be deploying. For example, if you ran sw-precache on the root of the application, it would try to cache lots of TypeScript files that you aren't even going to deploy. So ng serve isn't going to do you a lot of good.

> **Note**   One other thing about this project. It's written in TypeScript, a language created by Microsoft that compiles to JavaScript. TypeScript is a superset of the JavaScript syntax you've been using all along. What that means is that although every example you've seen so far is just JavaScript, it is also valid TypeScript. So don't let TypeScript intimidate you if you haven't used it before. It's likely, however, that you won't even see any TypeScript with what you're doing because you're not planning to change the actual application. Your job here is to be stealthy and tactical, trying to upgrade the app in place and get out before anyone notices. If you end up knee deep in TypeScript, call for reinforcements because something has gone terribly wrong.

Instead of running the app with resources served from memory, you need to actually build the app and work with the a dist directory. So at this point all of your npm packages should be finished downloading. Run the following command in the Movies-Finder directory:

```
npm run build --prod --aot
```

When this is finished and if all goes well, you'll see the dist directory in the project root. You can use your trusty http-server in this directory to run the app locally. Before you do, though, let's go ahead and set up sw-precache.

Setting Up sw-precache

The first thing you need for sw-precache is to install it via npm:

```
npm install --save-dev sw-precache
npm install --save sw-toolbox
```

You're going to be using sw-toolbox shortly, so you might as well install it while you're installing things. Let's create your sw-precache-config.js file first to let sw-precache know what you want it to cache. If you think back to Chapter 4, you did this very same thing.

```
module.exports = {
  navigateFallback: '/index.html',
  stripPrefix: 'dist',
  root: 'dist/',
  staticFileGlobs: [
    'dist/index.html',
    'dist/**.js',
    'dist/**.css'
  ]
};
```

Save that block in your config file in the root of the app. This is telling sw-precache that you want any route that it can't find to use index.html instead of that route. All of your files are in the dist directory, so you can strip that prefix and give your config that value for the root property. Then you want to tell sw-precache which files to cache. That

will include index.html as well as all of the .js and .css files. All of these files will
end up in the cache. Again, this won't help the first load, but all repeat visits should be
much faster.

The next step is to go to the package.json file in the root of the app. This not only
contains all of the dependencies for npm to install, but it also has a list of scripts to run,
like npm start, npm build, etc. Here you can add another one to build your pre-cache
file. You need to tell sw-precache about your config file and where to build the resulting
service worker. So in the scripts object, include the following property:

"pre-cache": "sw-precache --root=dist --config=sw-precache-config.js"

When you run npm run pre-cache, this command will create the service worker file
in the dist directory and point the config file. Go ahead and type npm run pre-cache
and check out the dist directory to see what you've got.

If all went as planned, you should see service-worker.js in that dist folder. If you
peek in there, it's a ton of code, very little of which you're concerned about. But the first
line of code should show you all of the files that are going to get pre-cached.

The last step is registering the service worker. You don't want to edit the index.html
file in the dist directory because that gets generated by the build process, which will
overwrite anything you change in there. Instead, go into the src directory to find that
index.html. Just above the ending </body> tag, let's register the service worker like so:

```
<script>
  if ('serviceWorker' in navigator) {
    navigator.serviceWorker.register('/service-worker.js').then((reg) => {
      console.log('Service Worker registered');
    }).catch((err) => {
      console.log('Service Worker registration failed: ', err);
    });
  }
</script>
```

This isn't anything you haven't seen before. The only part that's notable is the path
you're giving to register the service worker. Remember that this file gets re-generated
and put into the dist directory, so you need to point to where *that* service worker will be
in relation to the dist/index.html file.

You should be all set to try this out. In your terminal, run `npm run build --prod --aot` to generate and move the `index.html` file into the `dist` directory. Finally, building the app again requires a rebuild of the service worker file. Run `npm run pre-cache` again and you're ready to go.

Once that's finished, `cd` into the `dist` directory and run your `http-server`, then in Chrome, navigate to `http://localhost:8080`. You should see the Movies Finder app!

Pop open DevTools and move over to the *Application* tab, then down to the *Service Workers* section. There and in Figure 10-4, you should see your service worker installed and running.

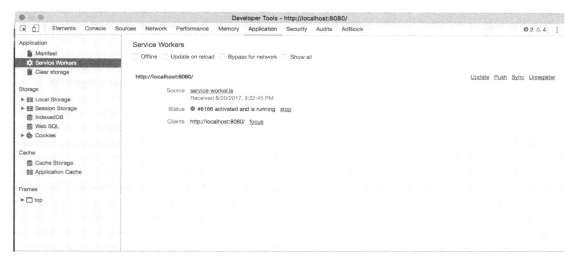

Figure 10-4. *Movies Finder now has a service worker*

Moving down to the *Cache Storage* section, you should now see some files being cached as well, just like in Figure 10-5.

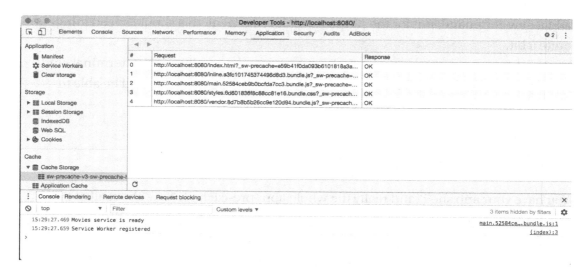

Figure 10-5. *Movies Finder is caching its JavaScript, CSS, and index.html files*

Now that you have that working, it's worth noting that the order that you build the app and run the pre-cache script is important. If you run pre-cache first, the bundle file names it will try to cache are going to be incorrect once you build the app because those files get renamed if any file in them changes. To ensure you always run these in the correct order, set up the `scripts` section of `package.json` to run them sequentially:

```
"scripts": {
    "ng": "ng",
    "start": "ng serve",
    "build": "ng build --prod --aot && npm run pre-cache && cd dist &&
http-server",
    "test": "ng test",
    "lint": "ng lint",
    "e2e": "ng e2e",
    "pre-cache": "sw-precache --root=dist --config=sw-precache-config.js"
  }
```

This will allow you to just type `npm run build` in the terminal and the app will build, `sw-precache` will run using the config file, the directory will change to `dist`, and launch your server. Once you're ready to deploy the app somewhere, you'll need to edit that or add a new command, but for the purposes of development, this should speed things up quite a bit.

If your server is still running, stop it, go to the app's root directory in terminal, and type `npm run build`. It will take a few seconds, but at the end you should be able to navigate to `http://localhost:8080` and you'll be all set.

Caching All the Things

You have your app shell (and really the whole app) pre-cached. Now about all of those images and API calls. You can cache the dynamic files with `sw-toolbox`. You don't want to edit the service worker directly, though, because it's a generated file and you'd lose those changes when you run `precache` again. Luckily for you, the `sw-precache` config works well with `sw-toolbox` and will allow you to set up your dynamic caching without touching the service worker file.

Open the `sw-precache-config.js` file and add a new property called `runtimeCaching`:

```
runtimeCaching: [
    {
      urlPattern: '/*',
      handler: 'cacheFirst',
      options: {
        origin: 'tmdb.org',
        cache: {
          maxEntries: 100,
          name: 'movie-cache'
        }
      }
    },
    {
      urlPattern: '/*',
      handler: 'cacheFirst',
```

```
    options: {
      origin: 'themoviedb.org',
      cache: {
        maxEntries: 10,
        name: 'movie-cache'
      }
    }
  }
]
```

Once you have this in your config file, you can type npm run pre-cache in your terminal and you should see this at the bottom of the service-worker.js file in the dist directory:

```
toolbox.router.get("/*", toolbox.cacheFirst, {"origin":"tmdb.org","cache":{
"maxEntries":100,"name":"movie-cache"}});
toolbox.router.get("/*", toolbox.cacheFirst, {"origin":"themoviedb.org",
"cache":{"maxEntries":10,"name":"movie-cache2"}});
```

You've seen something like that before! This is going to cache all of your calls to tmdb.org, which is where all of these images originate from, and calls from themoviedb. org, which is where the movie data comes from. You didn't make any changes to the app's code, so there's no need to fully rebuild the app. If you still have the server running, clear out the application data using the *Clear Storage* section of DevTools. Reload the app a couple of times. On that second load, most of your calls should be coming from the service worker, so your DevTools should look something like Figure 10-6.

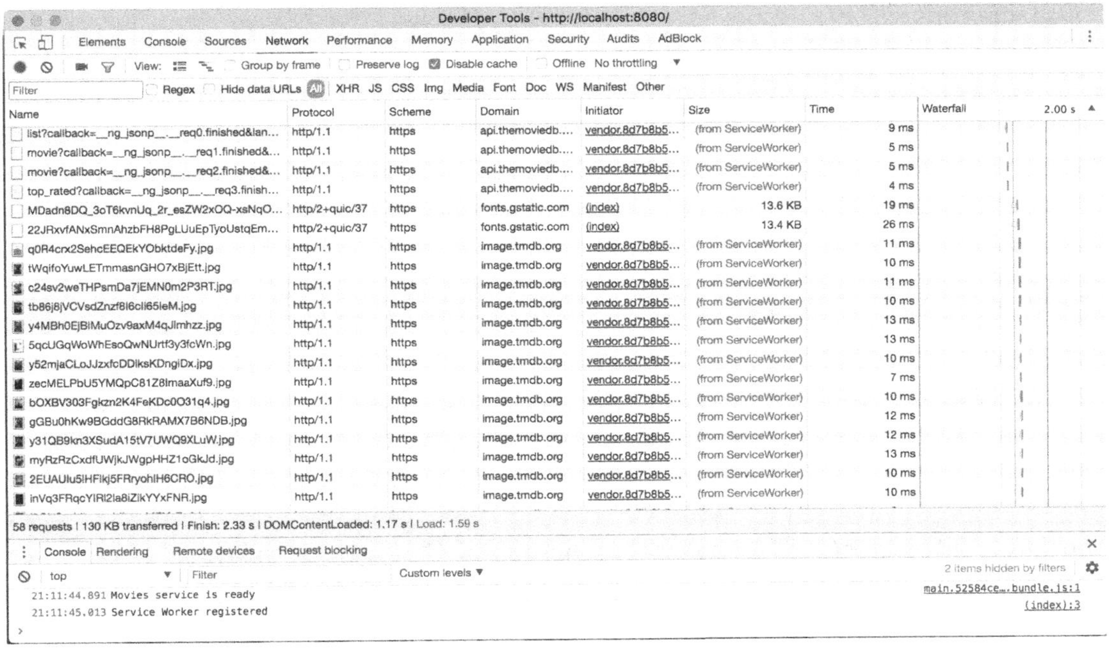

Figure 10-6. _The images and API calls for Movies Finder use the service worker cache now_

You're making steady progress. Your caching work is almost done. Open up `index.html` and you'll notice that there are two items in there that are being fetched from CDNs: a Bootstrap file and a jQuery script.

Neither of them are going to get pre-cached, so you can add them to `sw-precache-config.js` just like you did for the API calls and images, except this time you'll leave off the `maxEntries` and `name` options:

```
{
    urlPattern: '/*',
    handler: 'cacheFirst',
    options: {
      origin: 'bootstrapcdn.com'
    }
},
{
    urlPattern: '/*',
    handler: 'cacheFirst',
```

```
    options: {
      origin: 'jquery.com'
    }
}
```

With those two additions, the app should retain its styling even when your users are offline.

It won't do a lot of good to run a Lighthouse test on the project while you're hosting locally. So deploy to Firebase again to test your improvements. It's super easy, and I'll walk through the steps. But feel free to choose whatever hosting provider you'd like to deploy the app.

Deploying to Firebase

It's possible the steps here will change by the time you're reading this. If that's the case, check out the Firebase documentation (it's currently at `https://firebase.google.com/ docs/hosting/deploying`, but if the steps change, that URL could change, too, so just google "Firebase hosting").

The first step is to go to the Firebase console at `https://console.firebase.google.com`. Hopefully it looks something like in Figure 10-7. Sign in with your Google account and click the big *Add Project* button.

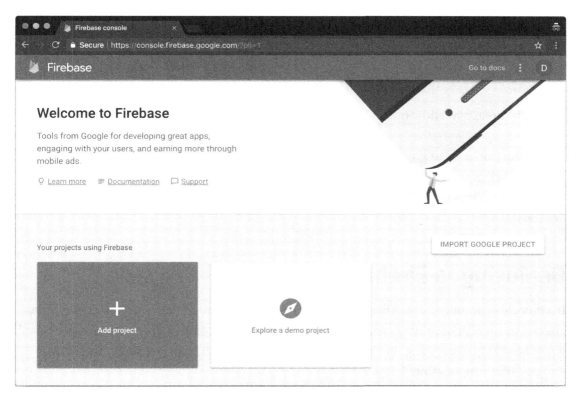

Figure 10-7. *The Firebase console*

Once you click that button, you can give your project a name. Let's name it *movie-finder-pwa*. After you name your app, you'll be taken to an overview screen. Scroll down a bit to see the *hosting* section and click *GET STARTED*, which will take you to another screen with another opportunity to click *GET STARTED*. Firebase will guide you through the steps of deploying your app, but the following is how Movies Finder was deployed:

1. Open your terminal and install the Firebase CLI using `npm i -g firebase-tools`.

2. Go to the app root in terminal and run `firebase login`, and type in your Google credentials.

3. Delete the existing `firebase.json` and `.firebaserc` files in the root of the project.

4. In the terminal, type in firebase init. Choose the "hosting" option like in Figure 10-8. This will create a new firebase.json and .firebaserc files.

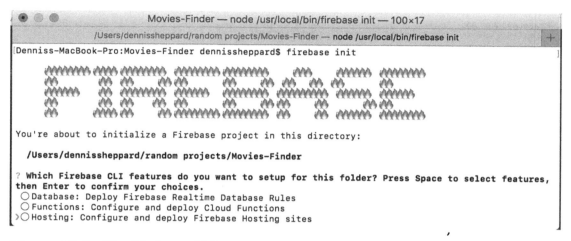

Figure 10-8. *The Firebase CLI*

5. Choose the Firebase project you created in the console.

6. Open the firebase.json file and paste in the following:

```
{
  "hosting": {
    "public": "dist"
  }
}
```

7. Back in the terminal, type firebase deploy.

Once you finish those steps, the app will be deployed to <whatever-app-name-you-chose>.firebaseapp.com. Run the app to make sure everything is working and then get Lighthouse going. Check out the results in Figure 10-9.

Results for: https://movie-finder-pwa.firebaseapp.com/
Aug 20, 2017, 10:15 PM CDT · ▸ Runtime settings

73
Progressive Web App

51
Performance

Progressive Web App

73

These audits validate the aspects of a Progressive Web App, as specified by the baseline PWA Checklist.

4 failed audits

▸ Page load is fast enough on 3G   ✓
First Interactive was found at 7,490 ms, however, the network request latencies were not sufficiently realistic, so the performance measurements cannot be trusted.

▸ User will not be prompted to Install the Web App   ✕
Failures: No manifest was fetched, Manifest start_url is not cached by a Service Worker.

▸ Is not configured for a custom splash screen   ✕
Failures: No manifest was fetched.

▸ Address bar does not match brand colors   ✕
Failures: No manifest was fetched, No `<meta name="theme-color">` tag found.

▸ 7 Passed Audits

▸ Manual checks to verify

Results for: https://movie-finder-pwa.firebaseapp.com/
Aug 20, 2017, 10:15 PM CDT · ▸ Runtime settings

Performance

51

These encapsulate your app's performance.

Metrics
These metrics encapsulate your app's performance across a number of dimensions.

| 749 ms | 1.5 s | 2.2 s | 3 s | 3.7 s | 4.5 s | 5.2 s | 6 s | 6.7 s | 7.5 s |

▸ First meaningful paint   6,750 ms

▸ First Interactive (beta)   7,490 ms

▸ Consistently Interactive (beta)   7,490 ms

▸ Perceptual Speed Index: 5,552 (target: < 1,250)   49

▸ Estimated Input Latency: 17 ms (target: < 50 ms)   100

Opportunities
These are opportunities to speed up your application by optimizing the following resources.

▸ Offscreen images   12,810 ms
1,120 KB

▸ Reduce render-blocking stylesheets   1,090 ms

Diagnostics
More information about the performance of your application.

▸ Critical Request Chains: 12

▸ User Timing marks and measures: 24

▸ 7 Passed Audits

Figure 10-9. *Lighthouse results after adding in the service worker and caching*

After adding the service worker in, you've improved the Lighthouse scores from 45 and 30 to 73 and 51. Not bad for just a little bit of work!

There's clearly some work to do in the performance department. Looks like there is a render blocking stylesheet. Let's take care of that and implement server push before you reevaluate Lighthouse.

Moving the Render-Blocking Stylesheet

Let's move all of the resources to the bottom of the `index.html` file so they don't block rendering. For your purposes, that's just the `https://bootswatch.com/superhero/bootstrap.min.css` file. You can't server push it because it's served from an external CDN. So let's move that line right beneath the `</app-root>` tag:

```
<link rel="preload" href="https://bootswatch.com/superhero/bootstrap.min.
css" as="style" onload="this.rel='stylesheet'">
```

Remember that telling the browser to preload that file will cause it to download right away, as early in the page's lifecycle as possible. The hope is that you can get that file early enough that it doesn't block any part of the rendering process. Last time we looked at this, you set an invalid media query that you changed to a valid one *onload*. Now you'll use a more concise trick that just changes the `rel` property to a stylesheet.

Note   Just like with a lot of these performance based changes, it's worth trying to load that file with and without preload to see which helps rendering the most.

Implementing Server Push

You'll recall that when the browser makes a request for your app, you have the ability to send files along with the `index.html` file so that the browser doesn't have to make additional requests for files you know it will need. But remember that you're focused on rendering speed. So you don't want to push everything you possibly can; you just want the files that impact rendering. For your purposes, that's going to be the CSS bundle and the two main JS bundles.

You'll need to rebuild the app to make sure you know what the bundle files are called so you can tell Firebase to push those to the client. After you build the app using ng build --prod --aot, open the firebase.json file. This is where you're going to add *link* headers containing the files you want Firebase to push. Let's look at what you want the config file to contain:

```
{
  "hosting": {
    "public": "dist",
    "headers": [
      {
        "source": "/",
        "headers": [
          {
            "key": "Link",
            "value": "<styles.6d601836f8c88cc81e16.bundle.css>;
            rel=preload;as=style,<vendor.8d7b8b5b26cc9e120d94.bundle.js>;
            rel=preload;as=script,<main.c1a2e8f5346f67c93597.bundle.js>;
            rel=preload;as=script"
          }
        ]
      }
    ]
  }
}
```

You've already used the config file to let Firebase know what directory you want to deploy. Now you can add a headers property that adds a key that tells Firebase what kind of header you want and then the value contains the file. That's it. You redeploy the app using firebase deploy in the terminal and you can measure again.

Note   Your bundle names will be different. If you're copying and pasting code, make sure you grab your actual bundle names!

If you'd like to try to push additional files, just add them to that string. It's definitely worth taking a little time to see if there's a noticeable performance improvement when pushing other files.

After deployment, if you clear the application data and reload, go over to the *Network* tab to verify the CSS bundle is getting pushed by looking in the *Initiator* column, like in Figure 10-10.

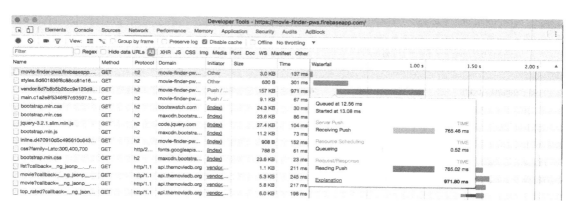

Figure 10-10.   *The Movies Finder bundles are getting pushed to the client*

So everything is looking really good here. You've pushed assets that you need early on and you moved the render blocking library file. Let's now look in Figure 10-11 to see if Lighthouse finds any improvements.

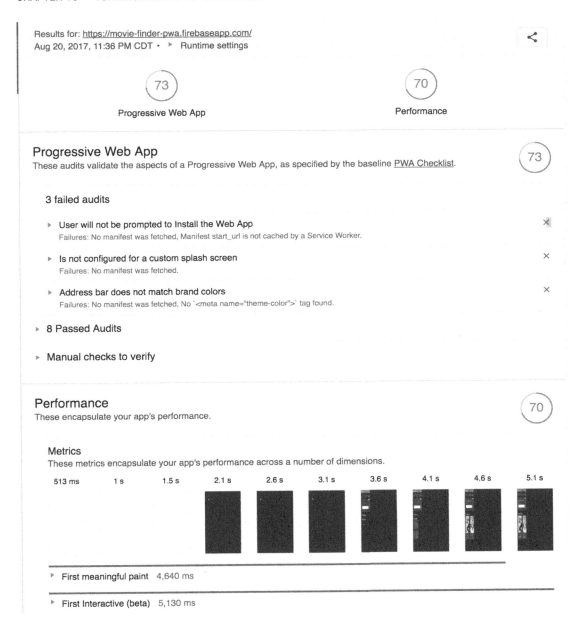

Figure 10-11. *Movies Finder Lighthouse scores after moving the Bootstrap file to the bottom of the index and preloading it, plus adding server push for the CSS bundle*

Hey look at that! The performance score went up almost 20 points! You can see that *something* shows up on the screen at just over two seconds, and you get a meaningful paint in under 5 seconds. We hit our original goal! Under 5 seconds isn't bad!

For our purposes here, that's all you're going to do for initial page load. But you should play with different server push options, try the Bootstrap file as a local resource instead of the CDN, and anything else you can think of. There will be additional tips to try in a couple of chapters, like code splitting and lazy loading. Remember that while using HTTP/2, large bundle files are an anti-pattern. So you could probably get that performance score up a bit more.

Note   If you're following along (of course you are!) and your Lighthouse score was different from the one posted above, remember that performance scores are always going to vary. Try running Lighthouse a handful of times to get a good sense of where your score ends up.

Now you'll shift your focus to a couple of the items in the PWA score. Lighthouse is yelling at you about splash screens and installing the app. And that means one thing: you need an app manifest! Let's get to it.

Adding the App Manifest

So that you can have a splash screen and allow the user to install your app on Android devices, you need to add an app manifest. This is a super straightforward process. You can borrow the manifest you used back in Chapter 6 and tweak it, or you can use a tool like `https://app-manifest.firebaseapp.com/`. There are a number of sites like this if you search around. This one allows you to fill in a few blanks to generate the file, and also allows you to upload an icon that it will downsize to create all of the app icons for you. This is a huge timesaver.

For the movie app, type in whatever info you'd like in those fields, and upload an icon to see them all generated. If you want to just pull down the `app-manifest` branch

of the https://github.com/dennissheppard/Movies-Finder repo, it will have all of the icons and the completed manifest file that you can also see here:

```
{
  "name": "Movie Finder",
  "short_name": "Movie Finder",
  "start_url": "index.html",
  "theme_color": "#df691a",
  "background_color": "#2b3e50",
  "display": "standalone",
  "description": "The only movie app you'll ever need",
  "icons": [
    {
      "src": "assets/app-icons/icon-72x72.png",
      "sizes": "72x72",
      "type": "image/png"
    },
    {
      "src": "assets/app-icons/icon-96x96.png",
      "sizes": "96x96",
      "type": "image/png"
    },
    {
      "src": "assets/app-icons/icon-128x128.png",
      "sizes": "128x128",
      "type": "image/png"
    },
    {
      "src": "assets/app-icons/icon-144x144.png",
      "sizes": "144x144",
      "type": "image/png"
    },
```

```
  {
    "src": "assets/app-icons/icon-152x152.png",
    "sizes": "152x152",
    "type": "image/png"
  },
  {
    "src": "assets/app-icons/icon-192x192.png",
    "sizes": "192x192",
    "type": "image/png"
  },
  {
    "src": "assets/app-icons/icon-384x384.png",
    "sizes": "384x384",
    "type": "image/png"
  },
  {
    "src": "assets/app-icons/icon-512x512.png",
    "sizes": "512x512",
    "type": "image/png"
  }
],
"prefer_related_applications": false
}
```

There are a couple of properties I've left off, like related_applications and orientation because you have no related apps here, and orientation can be anything for this particular app.

Now you need to include a reference to the manifest in your index.html. Place the following line as the last line of the <head> tag:

```
<link rel="manifest" href="/app-manifest.json">
```

The last step for the manifest is to include a reference to the manifest file in the angular-cli.json file. That file tells the build process what you need to copy over to the dist folder. Add your manifest to the assets array like so:

```
"assets": [
        "assets",
        "favicon.ico",
        "app-manifest.json"
    ]
```

Your manifest should be all set, and you can check on it in just a moment. First, there was one other suggestion Lighthouse had having to do with a theme color meta tag. This will make the address bar match the app's colors on browsers that support that meta tag. The goal here is to give users a completely immersive experience. You just need to throw the following line into the <head> of the index.html file:

```
<meta name="theme-color" content="#df691a"/>
```

Obviously you can make the color there whatever you'd like; this one just matches the manifest. So now you can build the app and run it locally to make sure the manifest is in place. Check in DevTools under the *Application* tab and you should see something like Figure 10-12.

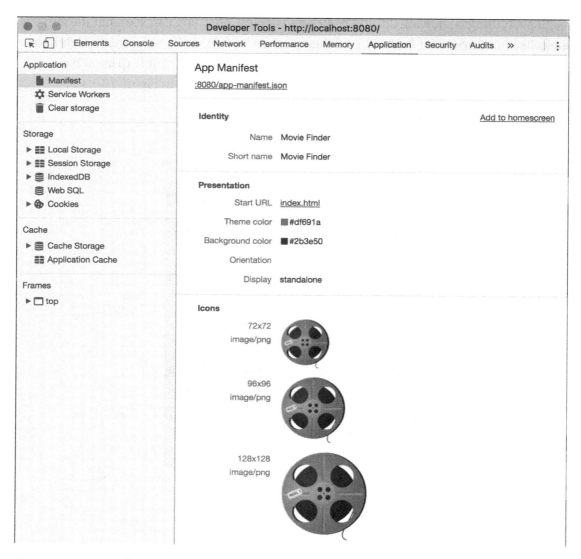

Figure 10-12. *The app manifest should be visible in DevTools*

Note   It's possible that when you first click on the *Manifest* section on the left side of the *Applications* tab that you won't see your manifest info on the right. There appears to be a bug in Chrome DevTools that requires you to close DevTools and re-open them before the manifest appears.

If everything is showing up, you're all set to deploy. First, you can see what the app looks like on Chrome for Android, and then you can look to see if you've made Lighthouse happy. Just run `firebase deploy` and let it do some work. If you're able to launch your app on Android, you should see some pretty cool stuff, as shown in Figure 10-13.

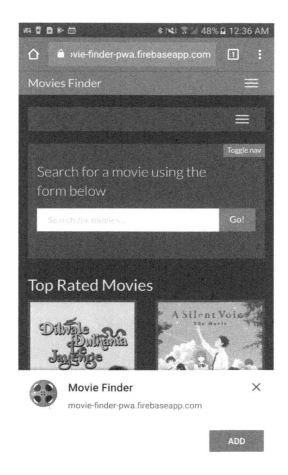

Figure 10-13. *Android is asking if you'd like to add your app to the home screen*

This is excellent! Notice that not only did Android prompt to install the app on its own, but that Chrome address bar matching your own nav bar is absolutely *sick*!

Once you add the app and launch it from the device home screen, you're greeted by the lovely splash page seen in Figure 10-14.

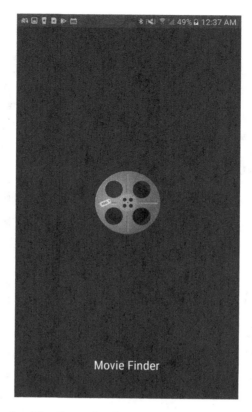

Figure 10-14. *The Movies Finder splash page, courtesy of the app manifest*

The splash page looks fantastic here. It's almost a shame that you only see it for a split second before the app launches and you see what's in Figure 10-15.

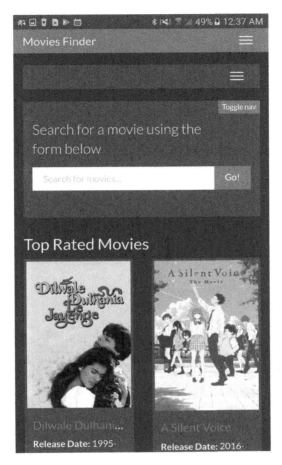

Figure 10-15. *Chrome's address bar disappears because of the standalone display property in the manifest*

You currently have `standalone` for the display property, but try out the different properties to see what you like for the app.

Now that you've seen how great the app is looking, let's see if you've made Lighthouse as happy as Chrome appears to be in Figure 10-16.

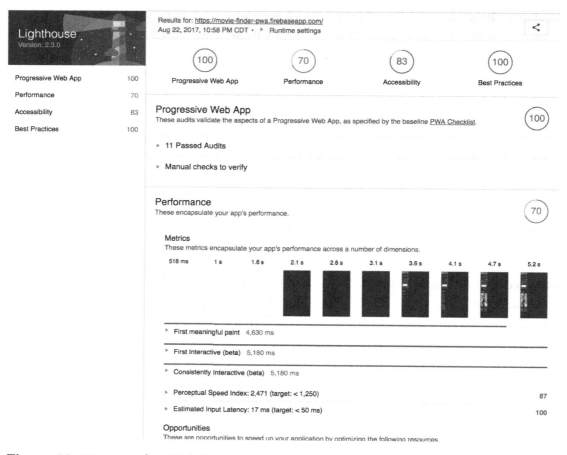

Figure 10-16. *A perfect Lighthouse PWA score!*

It looks like you've made Lighthouse *very* happy. You did it: a perfect PWA score! You can expand that section and see what you've accomplished. But that's not all, because now you're actually looking at the other couple of Lighthouse sections as well. You're following all of the best practices already, but each item in that list is straightforward to fix if you're seeing anything different. That's a fairly high accessibility score, too, though there are a couple of items to work on there.

You have yourself an actual, live, genuine PWA!

Thoughts on Movies Finder Performance

We set out knowing that the Lighthouse Performance score was going to be a steep hill to climb. There are a couple of factors working against us here. One is that the vendor bundle is really big. Angular is a relatively heavy framework, and as you'll see in the next chapter, of the current crop of popular frameworks, it is the bulkiest and gives developers the least amount of time to work with for optimizing time to first meaningful paint.

The second factor working against us is that the way the app functions leads to pulling down a lot of images on the home page. If you're super curious, you might find that if you take away all of those images and render just the actual app shell, you can boost that Performance score up into the mid 80s. That would require changing the functionality of the site, though, which would not only require some Angular knowledge, but is out of scope of our focus here.

It's also worth pointing out that the app uses two not-insignificant JavaScript files just to have the mobile menu appear on click. Those files are the JS used for Bootstrap (`bootstrap.min.js`) and jQuery. The version of jQuery in this repo is a slightly slimmed down version than the original, but it's still about 100KB of JavaScript just to have the menu appear.

So there are a number of things you could do really boost that score up:

1. Write a custom JS handler to show the menu on mobile, thereby eliminating 100KB of JavaScript.

2. Inline the styles needed to render the app shell and defer the need for the entire Bootstrap theme.

3. Change the functionality of the app so the user can click a button to see the most popular and newest movies, rather than automatically loading them. Or only show the top three of each section.

There are surely additional things you can do to squeeze every drop of performance out of this app. So give it a shot and see what you're capable of. Post your best performance scores in the pirate app comments, and if you can get into the 80s, let us know what you did to achieve it!

Looking Ahead

In this chapter, you focused on optimizing your Lighthouse scores, and you achieved those goals using much of what you learned in previous chapters. In the next chapter, you're going to rewind to the creation of apps using various popular front-end frameworks and see how they can get you started on the right PWA foot out of the box.

Before you move on, though, you may have noticed there were a couple of features you didn't use in the Movies Finder app. And because you're obviously itching to take on such a challenge (and you haven't been assigned any homework up to this point!), here is a very open-ended exercise for you to try.

BACKGROUND SYNC AND PUSH NOTIFICATIONS EXERCISE

There is undoubtedly an opportunity in this Movies Finder app to use background sync and push notifications. And so it is your mission to come up with the most creative way to do so.

1. Fork the `https://github.com/dennissheppard/Movies-Finder` repo.

2. Make sure you use the `app-manifest` branch so you have a service worker and app manifest in place.

3. Come up with a creative way to use background sync and/or push notifications. Remember, to use push notifications, you need to set up a server like you did in Chapter 7.

4. If you host your solution somewhere, comment about it on the pirate app comments section or on the `https://github.com/dennissheppard/Movies-Finder` issue tracker! Or at the least, share your ideas with everyone else.

Hint: It is worth noting that to use background sync, you will obviously need to make changes to the service worker file. But as I talked about earlier in this chapter, you can't directly edit that file because it's generated by the build process. So in order to extend the generated service worker with your custom changes, you'll need to utilize the `sw-precache importScripts` option in the configuration file. You can put your service worker-specific background sync and push notification code in separate JS files and import them via configuration. Don't forget to include those files in the `angular-cli.json` build configuration too, so they get deployed!

If you're stuck, you could use Jake Archibald's *Offline Wikipedia* app as inspiration. Check out the repo here: `https://github.com/jakearchibald/offline-wikipedia`. It's a great example of an offline app that notifies users when a previously un-cached article is available for reading. You can apply that same concept to the Movies Finder detail pages, showing a friendly offline message allowing the user to sign up for push notifications to let them know when the app is back online with a link to the route they were trying to view.

That's definitely a challenge, but you're absolutely capable of crushing it! Or, go off on your own and see what you can come up with. No matter which direction you go, have fun, and good luck!

CHAPTER 11

PWAs From the Start

To this point, you've cobbled together a Pirate PWA piece by piece and you took a movie app and totally transformed it (at least in the eyes of Lighthouse and the PWA world). There's nothing devs love more, though, than starting a new project from scratch. Just mention the words "greenfield" or "starter kit" to a software developer and watch their eyes light up. So in this chapter I'll talk about creating a progressive web app even before you add in any application logic. To do that, I need to talk about the most popular frameworks and libraries in the JavaScript ecosystem today. While it is a completely valid option to stick with VanillaJS to write your JavaScript apps (just look at that beautiful pirate app, after all), nowadays it's probably most common to use some kind of library or framework. There are just too many advantages to using React or Angular or lots of others to completely and purposely avoid them. And now that PWAs are taking the world by storm, those frameworks and libraries are following suit by giving you a PWA with just a few keystrokes. In this chapter, I'll talk about those keystrokes by covering a handful of the PWA-friendly frameworks and libraries available today: React, the ultra popular library originating from Facebook; Preact, a smaller and faster React alternative; Vue.js, the tiny view-focused library that has really blown up in the past year; Angular, the revamped component-based solution from Google; and Ionic, the mobile-centric framework built on top of Angular.

In comparing and contrasting these libraries and frameworks, though, it's important to remember that none of them should be considered a better alternative over the others. Sometimes it comes down to deciding on the right tool for the job. A hammer isn't inherently better than a screwdriver. Other times it comes down to personal preference.

That being said, each solution I'll cover has pros and cons in the PWA world. I'll focus on the performance of each framework and library so that if you need to be performance obsessed, you know just how much each of these solutions is going to cost you on that first page load before you add any of your own code and logic.

© Dennis Sheppard 2017

D. Sheppard, *Beginning Progressive Web App Development*, https://doi.org/10.1007/978-1-4842-3090-9_11

Just like in the Movies Finder app, your goal is for the app to be interactive within five seconds on a 3G connection. So you can measure how much time each framework's starter template takes to load out of the box. By doing so, you can see how much time you have to work with after adding in your own code.

Note   These will not exactly be robust, scientific tests that would hold up to extreme scrutiny. The testing method is simply running Lighthouse three times on each generated PWA. If one of the three is obviously out of line with the other two scores, you can drop that one and run another test. Each PWA will be available for you to test, so if you want to set up something more in depth, you're welcome to do so. Tell the rest of us about it on the iPatch comment board or in the book's GitHub issues. I look forward to seeing if your results match what we're about to see!

Regardless of the results you find here, though, and regardless of the differences in each framework and library, one of the great things about them is that each one empowers developers to focus on building great applications from the start.

Note   This chapter will not be a tutorial for each library and framework. Instead, I'll outline how to create a PWA with each of these at project creation, and look at how much flexibility developers have given each solution with regards to rendering speed and PWA features.

React PWA

The first library I'm going to talk about is arguably the most popular JavaScript library today. React.js is a project from Facebook that focuses on the view portion of front-end applications. It touts composability and speed along with being backed by one of the largest tech companies in the world. The main concept behind React is the use of components and managing their state.

Creating a React App

It's easy to start a React app using the *Create React App* tool. And as a bonus all apps created via this tool are PWAs by default. Let's take a look at what this means.

To get started, create a new directory somewhere on your machine and run the following to see the results from Figure 11-1:

```
npm install -g create-react-app
create-react-app react-pwa
```

```
~/random projects/frameworkpwas — -bash
[Denniss-MacBook-Pro:frameworkpwas dennissheppard$ create-react-app react-pwa

Creating a new React app in /Users/dennissheppard/random projects/frameworkpwas/react-pwa.

Installing packages. This might take a couple of minutes.
Installing react, react-dom, and react-scripts...

yarn add v0.20.3
info No lockfile found.
[1/4] 🔍 Resolving packages...
[2/4] 🚚 Fetching packages...
[3/4] 🔗 Linking dependencies...
```

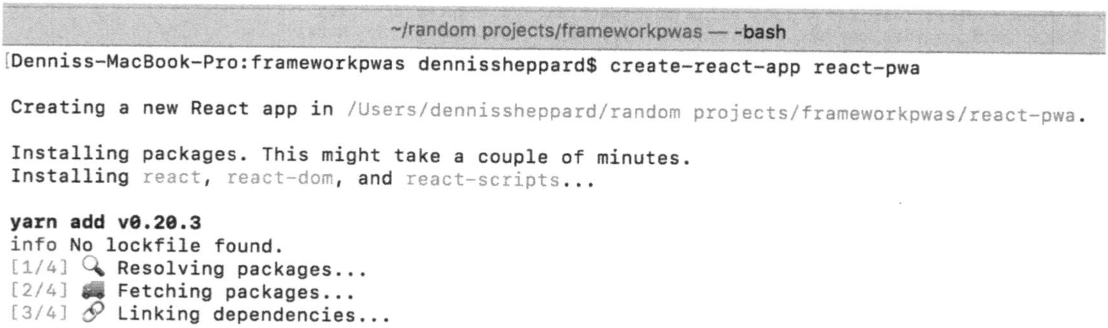

Figure 11-1. *The terminal when you run create-react-app react-pwa*

This is going to run for about a minute, installing various packages and dependencies. It will scaffold the app for you and generate a starter template that you can launch and see. When everything is finished running, just like in Figure 11-2, your terminal will tell you which yarn commands you can run with a helpful suggestion that you cd into the react-pwa directory and run yarn start.

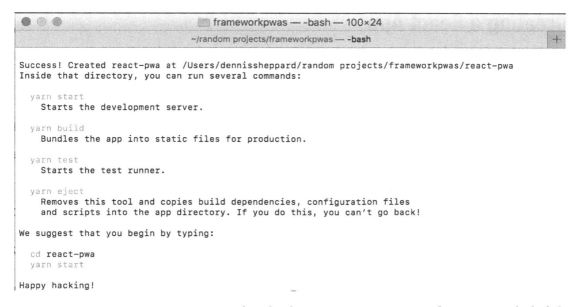

Figure 11-2. *Create React App is finished creating a project and even gives helpful hints on how to run it*

Let's go ahead and follow directions by running `yarn start`.

Note   The latest version of Create React App uses Yarn, a package management tool much like npm. Yarn was also created by Facebook, so it's a natural fit that the React setup would use it.

This launches a dev server on port 3000 and opens the corresponding web page. You're greeted with a warm welcome to React and instructions on which file to edit to make changes. You won't be making any changes, but let's check out DevTools and see if you can spot a service worker, an app manifest, and if any caching is happening right out of the box.

Open up DevTools and choose the *Application* tab. You can see right away that you have an app manifest. It defines theme colors, has names, a display property, and an app icon. Only the 192px icon is visible here, so you can already tell that Android won't show the install prompt to users. Lighthouse will double check that for you. Let's move on to the service worker section.

It's empty. Looks like no service worker is getting registered for this created app. And because there's no service worker, obviously there's nothing cached here, either. You were promised a PWA right out of the box. What's going on here?

Configuring the Service Worker

If you look at the README.md file in the root of the app, there is an entire section on Progressive Web Apps with a wealth of information on how the *Create React App* setup deals with service workers and other PWA features.

Reading through this, you learn that the way the *Create React App* is configured, the service worker only gets registered for production builds. You can also see that sw-precache is baked into the production build process. That's great news!

Note   There are some valid explanations here for why the offline functionality is only enabled in production builds. Developers who aren't as familiar with service workers as you are would really be thrown off as to why all of their changes are ignored during development. And let's be honest, even you might forget that your service worker cached that one JS file that's nestled four levels deep in your app's directory structure.

Further reading shows that there is support for runtime caching, but the process is slightly different from what you're used to:

> *By default, the generated service worker file will not intercept or cache any cross-origin traffic, like HTTP API requests, images, or embeds loaded from a different domain. If you would like to use a runtime caching strategy for those requests, you can [run npm] eject and then configure the runtime- Caching option in the SWPrecacheWebpackPlugin section of webpack.con- fig.prod.js.*
>
> —Create React App, README.md

Eject? That sounds… interesting. What's going on here is that the *Create React App* setup is trying to streamline everything for you. You're in the pilot's seat, but the plane is on auto-pilot. By running npm run eject, it takes you out of the normal workflow and shows you all of your configuration files. Try running it and you can see you now have a config directory with the Webpack configuration files mentioned above.

So you still have control of your service worker and your app caching strategy, but the details are abstracted away from you. If you're more comfortable manually writing your service worker and caching everything yourself, that's absolutely doable.

Moving on in the README.md, you can also see information on the app manifest, but there's nothing really insightful here. You're likely pretty well-versed on app manifests by this point.

Essentially, in order to test your service worker, you need to build and run the app much like the way you did the Movies Finder app in the last chapter. So let's do that because you want to see the service worker in action and want to run a Lighthouse assessment to really see what you're working with here.

Running and Building the React App

In order to create your production build of this starter template app, you just need to run yarn build in the root directory. That will tell you that an optimized production build is getting created, and everything is now in a build directory. This is essentially the same thing as the dist directory from last chapter. Let's peek in there in Figure 11-3 and see what you've got.

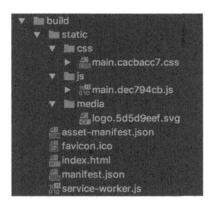

Figure 11-3. *The build directory you want to serve up contains your JavaScript bundle, some CSS, a service worker, a manifest, and the index.html file*

Looks like everything you could possibly need is in there. Let's go ahead and cd into that directory in the terminal and run http-server. Go to localhost:8080 in Chrome and you should see the same React welcome screen.

Note   If you're following along in lockstep from last chapter, when you go to `localhost:8080` you might see the Movies Finder app. That's because of the service worker caching. Just go to the *Application* tab in DevTools and clear out everything.

If you open up DevTools, now you'll see that a service worker is registered, activated, and running. Let's hop down to the *Cache Storage* (you may need to right-click and choose *Refresh Caches*) and in there you can see that sw-precache has already cached the `index.html` file, along with the JS and CSS bundles, and the main logo on the page.

Feel free to explore how the code is structured here, but you can see that you should have a really solid PWA foundation to build on for the next time you want to create a React app. Let's do a little performance measuring.

Deploying and Measuring Your React PWA

You don't particularly want to measure the performance of an app when serving from localhost. So let's throw these starter PWAs up on Firebase so you can poke and prod them remotely. If you'd like to deploy to your own remote server, feel free to follow the steps outlined in the previous chapter when you deployed the Movies Finder app to Firebase. Alternatively, you can just look here for the React PWA deployment: `https://react-pwa-bd5da.firebaseapp.com`.

Let's open that up and run Lighthouse on it and see what's what. See the results in Figure 11-4.

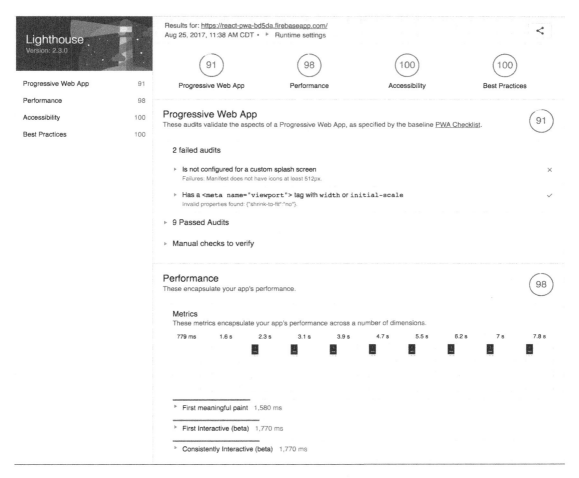

Figure 11-4. *React.js Lighthouse results for Create React App starter project*

Without adding any of your own code, the *Create React App* project gives really impressive scores. We knew that Lighthouse was going to complain about the manifest not having the right icon size, so the project got dinged for that one. There's another minor issue with a viewport meta tag. But those are easily fixable. Accessibility and Best Practices start out at 100s, which is excellent. All you have to do as a dev is not mess that up.

Now you get to performance. Your goal with any PWA is a Time to First Interactive on 3G in under five seconds. The way you'll compare these frameworks is by running Lighthouse three times and taking an average. As you can see in the screenshot, you got

1.77 seconds here, and the average of three runs ended up being 1.8 seconds. So this tells you that once you add in your own code, images, functionality, etc., you have 3.2 seconds to work with, as you can see in the fantastic little graph in Figure 11-5.

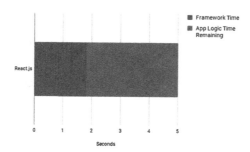

Figure 11-5. *The amount of time React.js takes to reach First Interactive without any application functionality*

Summary of React's PWA Effort

The setup of your React PWA was really easy. The *Create React App* made the developer experience really seamless and you were up in running in very little time. With perfect scores in Best Practices and Accessibility, it's a little surprising that the manifest and a meta tag kept the project from being perfect in the PWA section. That's a particularly minor gripe, though, and a 98 in performance while only using 1.8 seconds seems impressive.

Of course, you don't have much of a frame of reference. So now let's move on to the next library, Preact.js.

Preact PWA

Preact is an incredibly small library. It comes in at just 3KB. It's positioned as a lighter, faster alternative to React. It aims to be mostly compatible with the React API, but some features were purposely left out for either performance reasons or were just out of scope of Preact's goal.

Jason Miller is the creator of Preact, and the project has around 100 contributors on GitHub. While Preact has only been around for a couple of years, it's already used by some big name companies like Uber, Pepsi, and The New York Times.

Preact CLI

The Preact CLI claims a "100 Lighthouse score right out of the box." You saw that React was close to that, but you'll see shortly if Preact lives up to that claim. There is a section of the Preact website dedicated specifically to PWAs and reasons for why Preact is a good choice for one. I already discussed how small the library is, so that's obviously going to help performance.

Let's follow the same steps as with React. In fact, the process is almost identical:

```
npm install -g preact-cli
preact create preact-pwa
```

Just like with React, this will install all of the necessary dependencies and get everything scaffolded out for you, as you can see in Figure 11-6.

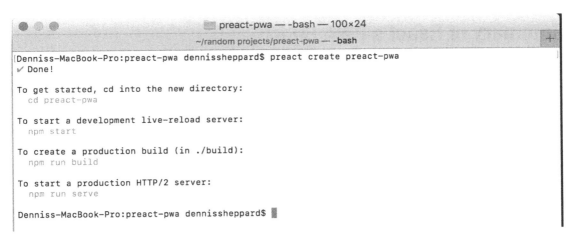

Figure 11-6. *Preact installs all of the dependencies and creates a project structure for you, and it gives instructions on how to run the app*

This looks a lot like what React does, but here you have *npm* instead of *Yarn*. Also, that last line is interesting. You have the ability to run an HTTP/2 server out of the box with the production build. That should give you an app manifest and service worker functionality. Let's run it and check it out!

Running the Built-in Preact HTTP/2 Server

In the terminal, cd into the newly created *preact-pwa* project and then type npm run serve. You'll be prompted with a password to set up the SSL certs for the HTTP/2 server. You can also catch the precaching already happening via the CLI, like in Figure 11-7.

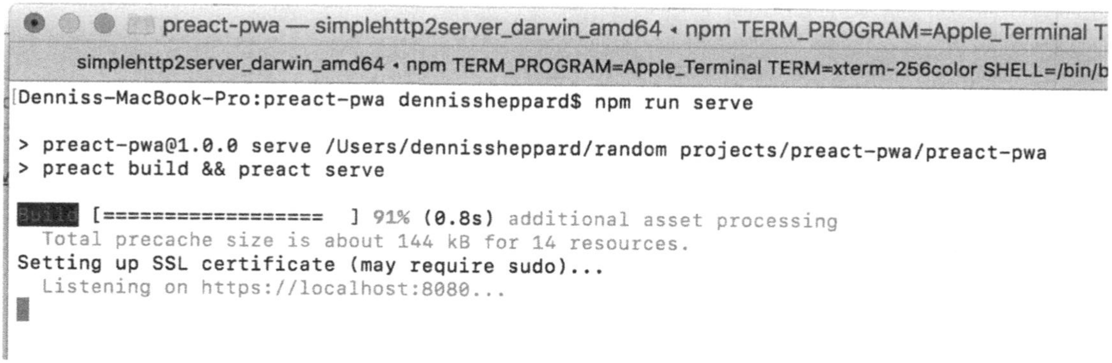

```
preact-pwa — simplehttp2server_darwin_amd64 • npm TERM_PROGRAM=Apple_Terminal T
simplehttp2server_darwin_amd64 • npm TERM_PROGRAM=Apple_Terminal TERM=xterm-256color SHELL=/bin/b
[Denniss-MacBook-Pro:preact-pwa dennissheppard$ npm run serve

> preact-pwa@1.0.0 serve /Users/dennissheppard/random projects/preact-pwa/preact-pwa
> preact build && preact serve

Build [==================  ] 91% (0.8s) additional asset processing
  Total precache size is about 144 kB for 14 resources.
Setting up SSL certificate (may require sudo)...
  Listening on https://localhost:8080...
```

Figure 11-7. *The Preact CLI is pre-caching assets before you've configured a single thing*

Now go to localhost:8080 and open up DevTools and you'll discover not only an app manifest, but also an installed and activated service worker. You see above that the CLI is precaching 14 resources, and you can verify that in the *Cache Storage* section of DevTools. There are a handful of icons in there, as well as the app manifest, the index.html file, and some JavaScript and CSS files. If you had DevTools open before loading the app, move over to the *Network* tab and you're in for a real treat. If not, just clear out everything with the *Clear storage* section of the *Application* tab and reload.

In Figure 11-8, the *Network* tab shows that not only do you have an HTTP/2 server, but it's using server push by default. You're in PWA heaven!

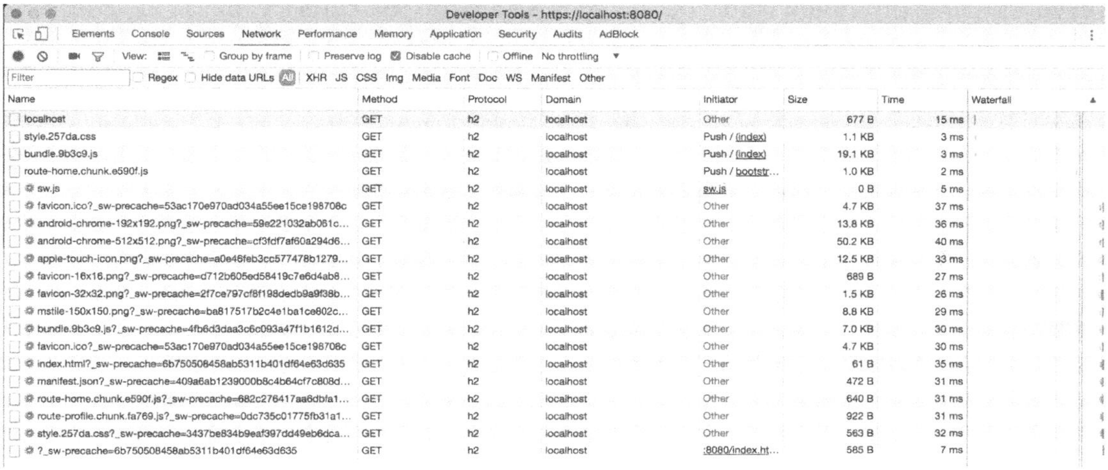

Figure 11-8. *HTTP/2 and server push right out of the box*

Not only do you have all of these PWA goodies, but the setup was super easy. You typed in four short commands, and you're given a fully featured PWA starter template.

Before you get too carried away, though, once you deploy let's talk about something that isn't quite as easy: runtime caching.

Preact CLI Plugins

Runtime caching with React wasn't quite as straightforward as the rest of the process (remember the `eject` command?), and that's also the case with the Preact CLI. The service worker process is entirely abstracted away, so much so that you can't simply eject in this case.

Instead, you need to install a separate npm package to configure `sw-precache`. If you want to try this out now, the process isn't complex, it's just quite a departure from how easy the rest of the Preact CLI was. Let's take a look.

The first step is to run

```
npm install --save-dev preact-cli-sw-precache
```

Next, you need to create a file in the root of the project called `preact.config.js` and import the package you just installed and set up your `sw-precache` config:

```
const swPrecache = require('preact-cli-sw-precache');

export default function (config) {
  const precacheConfig = {
    staticFileGlobs: [
      '/**.css',
      '/**.html',
      '/assets/**.*',
      '/**.js'
    ],
    stripPrefix: 'app/',
    runtimeCaching: [{
      urlPattern: '/',
      handler: 'networkFirst'
    }]
  };

  return swPrecache(config, precacheConfig);
}
```

When you build with this file in the root of the project, you can customize your `sw-precache` just like you did with the Movies Finder app. So while there are additional steps to have this type of functionality, it's really not so bad.

The last step to checking out the Preact PWA is to run it through the Lighthouse test battery. You don't really want to run your Lighthouse tests locally. So you will deploy it to Firebase just like you did with React. You'll lose your built-in server push in that process, but you're taking the rest of your built-in Preact PWA goodies and running away with them.

Running Lighthouse on Firebase-Deployed Preact

You want to deploy just like you have before, so you'll follow those same steps. Just like last time, if you don't want to go through the deployment process just to see some Lighthouse scores, you can check out the deployed version here: `https://preact-pwa-27be0.firebaseapp.com/`.

It should come as no surprise given everything I've discussed about Preact, but the Lighthouse scores are absolutely phenomenal. Check out Figure 11-9.

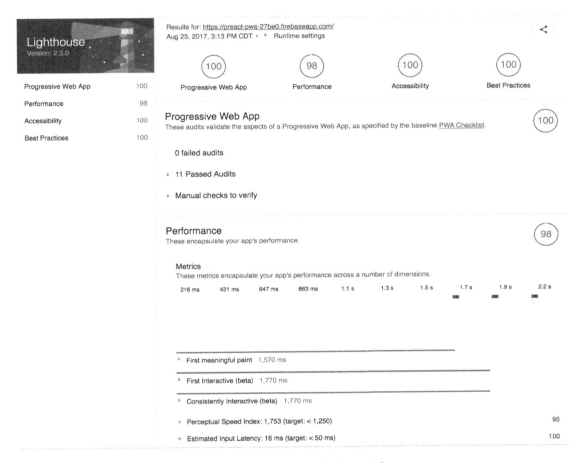

Figure 11-9. Preact achieves Lighthouse perfection. Almost.

With no configuration and in a matter of seconds, you have an app that is as close to Progressive Web App perfection as you could reasonably expect to get. It checks off every PWA box, implements each best practice, and includes every accessibility recommendation. These scores are so good, it's almost annoying that you can't somehow grab those extra two points from the performance score. We'll take it anyway, though.

After a few runs of Lighthouse, Preact performed at an average of 1.745 seconds in Time to First Interactive, just barely beating out React. You can see just how close they are in the return of the nifty graph in Figure 11-10.

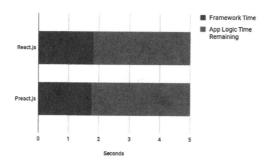

Figure 11-10. *Preact narrowly edges out React in Time to First Interactive*

Summary of Preact's PWA Effort

This performance score will give your app about 3.25 seconds to load before hitting the 5 second Time to First Interactive goal. For all practical purposes, this is the same as React. As for the PWA scores, the couple of items keeping React from achieving the perfect 100 are quickly and easily remedied, but the Preact setup took care of them for you.

Both solutions required a bit of extra configuration to get runtime caching (and any other service worker features) in place, which is a minor concern, but it's really only a couple of extra steps.

These are both great solutions. So when choosing between the two, for PWA purposes, your decision should really just come down to a personal preference.

One thing to keep in mind is that both of these libraries deal specifically with the view layer of your application. Things like managing application and model state, data fetching, and routing all require additional libraries. Just something to consider. The next library I'll discuss has the same consideration, but is blowing up in popularity. Let's see how it measures up.

Vue.js PWA

Vue.js is a JavaScript framework that has a strong focus on being light, fast, and simple. It's focus is on the view layer of applications, but is capable of powering large front-end heavy applications if it has some helper libraries to go along with it.

It's another relatively new-on-the-scene solution but already has well over 100 contributors to the project, and it has exploded in popularity over the last year or so.

On the PWA side of things, Vue provides a set of templates that allow developers to have options around what kind of project they would like to start. One of these templates is a PWA template that you can find here: `https://github.com/vuejs-templates/pwa`. Much like React and Preact, let's follow the instructions and spin up a project.

Vue CLI and PWA Creation

Run the following commands in your terminal in whatever directory you'd like to put your Vue PWA project:

```
npm install -g vue-cli
vue init pwa vue-pwa
```

Note   That last command looks a little convoluted. But the pwa part specifies which template to use, while `vue-pwa` is the name of the project.

This setup requires quite a bit more configuration. There are about nine questions the CLI asks you before you're ready to go. Most of them are quick and painless, so you can breeze through them.

Once you `cd` into the project root directory, you need to run `npm install`. That's different from the previous two solutions that installed all of the needed dependencies for you. Just one extra step, though, and it goes relatively quickly.

After the install finishes, you could either run the dev server or create a production build. The dev build doesn't create a service worker, though, so just like with *Create React App*, you'll want to run a production build and serve your app from the newly created folder. So ignore what the terminal tells you and instead run `npm run build` in the root directory.

Nothing fancy here; it simply creates a `dist` directory. Let's take a look in there (Figure 11-11) before deploying and testing with Lighthouse.

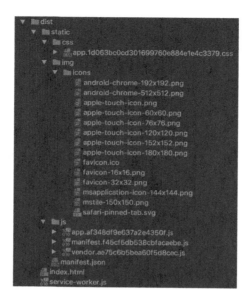

Figure 11-11. *The dist directory contains the app manifest, a service worker, and all of the needed icons*

What the Deployed Vue PWA Offers

It looks like you should have all of the major parts of your PWA, so let's go ahead and deploy instead of running locally. You can check out the service worker and manifest once everything is up on Firebase. If you'd like, you can see the base starter template deployed up on Firebase here: `https://vue-pwa-c7515.firebaseapp.com`.

Open that up and let's check out DevTools. You've got a service worker all ready to go and the manifest looks like it's in great shape. Let's go down to the *Cache Storage* and check out if you have pre-caching in Figure 11-12.

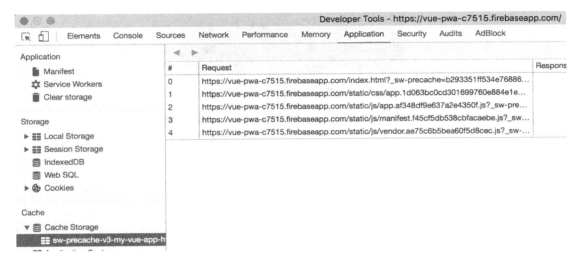

Figure 11-12. *The Vue.js PWA template gives you sw-precache out of the box*

So you have your service worker, an app manifest, and pre-caching. The only thing left to find out is how easy implementing runtime caching is.

Go back to the code and check out the `build` directory. In there you'll find a file called `webpack.prod.conf.js`. This contains all of the build configurations. Just like the other solutions, the Vue.js CLI build process is built on Webpack. You can edit this config file to add in runtime caching. Look for the following block of code:

```
// service worker caching
  new SWPrecacheWebpackPlugin({
    cacheId: 'vue-pwa',
    filename: 'service-worker.js',
    staticFileGlobs: ['dist/**/*.{js,html,css}'],
    minify: true,
    stripPrefix: 'dist/'
  })
```

You can add a `runtimeCaching` property in there that takes an array of objects with route patterns and caching strategies:

```
// service worker caching
  new SWPrecacheWebpackPlugin({
    cacheId: 'vue-pwa',
    filename: 'service-worker.js',
```

```
staticFileGlobs: ['dist/**/*.{js,html,css}'],
minify: true,
stripPrefix: 'dist/',
runtimeCaching: [
{
  urlPattern: "/*,
  handler: 'cacheFirst'
},
})
```

For Vue, there was no need to eject or install a plugin. You could just directly change the Webpack configuration. Nice and easy.

Running Lighthouse on Firebase-Deployed Vue

Now let's go ahead and run the Lighthouse tests and see where the Vue PWA template starts you off. The results are in Figure 11-13.

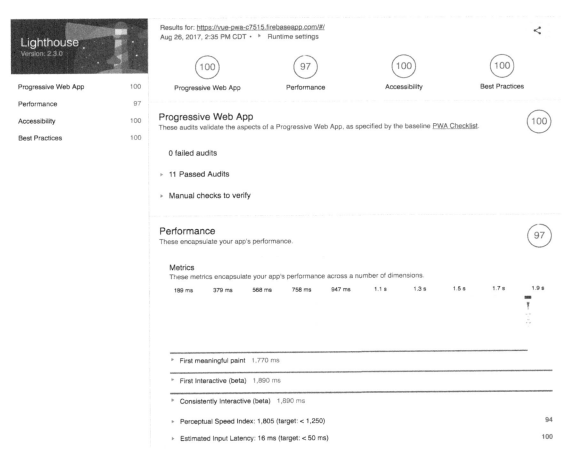

Figure 11-13. *Vue.js comes in with fantastic Lighthouse scores, perfect in three of four categories, with a near-perfect Performance score*

Vue looks to be just about perfect when it comes to Lighthouse. It trails React and Preact in the Performance category by just a single point. The Time to First Interactive was just a hair higher than those other two libraries, but the amount wouldn't be noticeable to users. For a comparison, check out Figure 11-14.

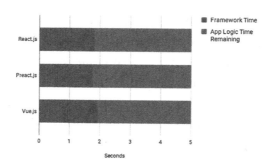

Figure 11-14. *The comparison of the three solutions so far is very consistent, with Vue trailing behind React by a few milliseconds, and Preact in the lead by an even smaller margin*

Vue leaves you just over three seconds to load up all of your own application logic and resources. There's less than a quarter of a second difference between Vue and Preact on a 3G connection, and with enough tests, it's possible that even that difference shrinks further.

Summary of Vue's PWA Effort

Vue had the most configuration needed to get set up so far, but that's not saying much. There's just a handful of questions asked at the beginning, and that could be nice for a little extra customization from the start. Additionally, Vue has made adding in runtime caching the easiest of the three solutions, with the configuration file already available for easy editing.

The next two frameworks you'll be looking at are at a disadvantage on paper. They're bigger frameworks with more capabilities. While these first three options are focused exclusively on the view layer of the application, Angular and Ionic (which is built on top of Angular) are full-fledged front-end frameworks. Let's see how Angular stacks up.

Angular PWA

Angular underwent a dramatic change in the last couple of years. AngularJS 1.x dominated front-end frameworks for a few years before React came on to the scene. The component-based model of React along with its virtual DOM abstraction lured developers away, showing some of the weaknesses of the AngularJS framework. Once ES6 finalized and TypeScript stormed onto the scene, the Angular team decided the

framework was due for a complete overhaul. What was formerly known as Angular 2 is now known as just Angular (the current version is Angular 5, and by the time you're reading this it's likely it could be even higher). Angular is not just an upgrade from AngularJS, it's a completely different framework.

Backed by Google, thousands of enterprise companies use Angular. It's a fully featured framework that not only takes care of the view layer, but has a much larger API that allows for robust change detection, front-end routing, support for observables via RxJS, and more.

You saw an Angular PWA in Chapter 10. But you gradually made that app a PWA rather than starting as one. Here the goal is to start from scratch.

Angular's Rocky PWA Start

Once upon a time, there was support for PWAs via a project called Angular Mobile: `https://mobile.angular.io/`. The site looks promising, and is completely PWA focused. However, at the time of this writing, that project is dead.

In its place is a project called *Angular Service Worker*. This is still a very new project, so it's still in beta, and there's not a lot of documentation yet. Let's see what we can squeeze out of it, though.

Let's get started by installing the Angular CLI and creating an app:

```
npm install -g @angular/cli
ng new angular-pwa
cd angular-pwa
```

This will create a new Angular project called angular-pwa. All of your packages and dependencies were installed, and you're ready to go.

The next step is to install the Angular Service worker:

```
npm install --save @angular/service-worker
ng set apps.0.serviceWorker=true
```

This will install the necessary files, and sets a flag inside of the `.angular-cli.json` file. From there, you need to create a configuration file that will allow you to customize your service worker. Create an empty file in the root of the project and call it `ngsw-manifest.json`. You don't need to add anything in there for static caching, as that's already taken care of for you. But for runtime caching, you can configure it like so:

```
"dynamic": {
  "group": [
    {
      "name": "angular-pwa",
      "urls": {
        "/*": { "match": "prefix" }
      },
      "cache": {
        "optimizeFor": "performance",
        "maxAgeMs": "360000000",
        "maxEntries": 10,
        "strategy": "lru"
      }
    }
  ]
}
```

At the moment, finding documentation for this is nearly impossible, and the properties don't seem to follow the standard ones you're used to in other projects. There are a few presentations on this file, but anything official seems to still be forthcoming. Hopefully, by the time you read this everything is well documented.

Building the Angular PWA

Luckily, the Movies Finder app was built with the Angular CLI, so you should already be familiar with the necessary build commands. You could run `ng serve`, and that will launch a server with all of your files served from memory. But you're more interested in what the production-ready package looks like, because that's when you get your service worker and your `ngsw-manifest.json`. So let's go ahead and build the project using `ng build --prod` and you'll deploy the resulting `dist` folder, which should now have your service worker in it. You'll find this brand new Angular PWA here: `https://angular-pwa-e74db.firebaseapp.com/`.

Running Lighthouse on Firebase-Deployed Angular

The relatively underwhelming PWA scores are shown in Figure 11-15.

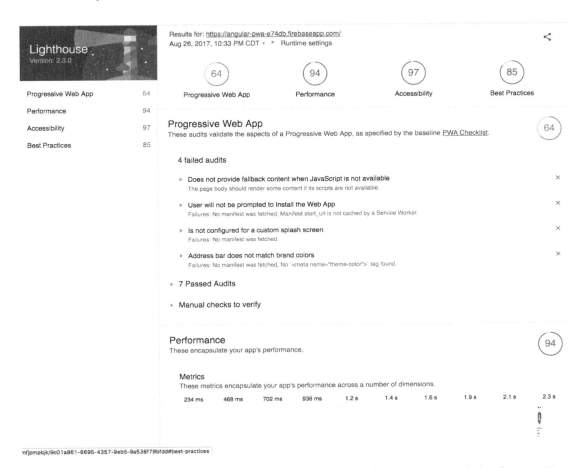

Figure 11-15. *Angular CLI falls short of producing the same out-of-the-box PWA experience as React, Preact, and Vue.js*

Given the fact that the Angular CLI didn't provide even a service worker out of the box, much less an app manifest, the PWA score isn't surprising. The Accessibility and Best Practices scores are decent, and at this point you're well equipped to get those scores up to 100s. What you have less control over is that Performance score. Thankfully, it's really solid, but it doesn't quite hit the same level as the other frameworks and libraries you've seen. A few points, though, shouldn't scare you away from using Angular. You can see in Figure 11-16 that Angular falls behind the rest of the pack.

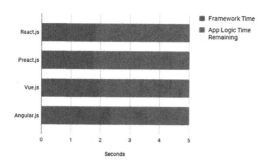

Figure 11-16. *Angular trails the other three solutions by almost half a second, but that's not the real issue with the PWA offering*

Summary of Angular's PWA Offering

The performance of Angular is surprisingly good considering the amount of features available in the framework. The real issue here is that Angular is such a major player in the front-end community, and has been for a long time, and yet at the moment there isn't much support for starting an Angular application as a PWA. It looks like improvements are coming, but the framework has clearly been passed by the other major solutions. Even more surprising is that Angular is a Google-backed project, and in the push for PWAs there is no bigger champion than Google.

Given this, you have to think that by the time you're reading this, Angular will get its PWA ducks in a row. As it stands at this moment, there is quite a bit of work to do to before Angular gets up to the level of React, Preact, or Vue when it comes to PWAs.

That should make the next and final framework all the more interesting. Ionic, which is built with Angular, promises devs a great PWA experience from a framework that's geared toward compiled native applications. Let's see what it's got.

Ionic PWA

Ionic is a framework built on top of Angular that focuses on building native mobile apps with front-end technologies. If you're familiar with Phone Gap, it's the same idea: leveraging Cordova to take a JavaScript application and make it native mobile-friendly.

Because that mission is closely aligned with PWAs, in late 2016, the Ionic team announced support for PWAs as well. If that support proves to be robust, it could be an alternative to starting a PWA project with Angular, since that's what's under the Ionic hood. Let's go through the installation process and see if it's able to improve on the Angular CLI experience.

Installing Ionic

The developer experience for setting up Ionic is definitely a pleasant one. There's robust documentation for just about everything, and the steps are on par with what you've seen for React, Preact, and Vue. To begin, just install the Ionic CLI and start up a project:

```
npm i -g cordova ionic
ionic start ionic-pwa
```

After running these commands, you'll be asked a couple of configuration questions like in Figure 11-17.

```
[Denniss-MacBook-Pro:ionic-pwa dennissheppard$ ionic start ionic-pwa          ]
[ ANNOUNCE ] Hi! Welcome to CLI 3.9.

          We decided to merge core plugins back into the main ionic CLI package. The
          @ionic/cli-plugin-ionic-angular, @ionic/cli-plugin-ionic1, @ionic/cli-plugin-cordova, and

          @ionic/cli-plugin-gulp plugins have all been deprecated and won't be loaded by the CLI
          anymore. We listened to devs and determined they added unnecessary complexity. You can
          uninstall them from your project(s).

          No functionality was removed and all commands will continue working normally. You may
          wish to review the CHANGELOG:
          https://github.com/ionic-team/ionic-cli/blob/master/CHANGELOG.md#changelog

          Thanks,
          The Ionic Team


? The Ionic CLI can automatically check for CLI updates in the background. Would you like to enable
[this? No                                                                     ]

? What starter would you like to use: blank
✔ Creating directory ./ionic-pwa - done!
[ INFO ] Fetching app base (https://github.com/ionic-team/ionic2-app-base/archive/master.tar.gz)
✔ Downloading - done!
[ INFO ] Fetching starter template blank
        (https://github.com/ionic-team/ionic2-starter-blank/archive/master.tar.gz)
✔ Downloading - done!
✔ Updating package.json with app details - done!
✔ Creating configuration file ionic.config.json - done!
[ INFO ] Installing dependencies may take several minutes!
> npm install
✔ Running command - done!
> git init
> git add -A
> git commit -m "Initial commit" --no-gpg-sign

♫♪ ♫♪  Your Ionic app is ready to go! ♫♪ ♫♪

Run your app in the browser (great for initial development):
  ionic serve

Run on a device or simulator:
  ionic cordova run ios

Test and share your app on a device with the Ionic View app:
  http://view.ionic.io


Next Steps:
Go to your newly created project: cd ./ionic-pwa
```

Figure 11-17. *Setting up a new Ionic project*

Just like with a couple of the other solutions you've looked at, there are different templates for developers to choose from to bootstrap the app. A lot of mobile applications have a tabbed interface, and Ionic will start you off with one of those out of the box if you'd like. For your PWA, though, you'll just choose the *Blank* template. Once everything is installed, you can cd into the project's directory.

Enabling the Ionic Service Worker

When building an Ionic app for production, you should get a service worker and an app manifest automatically. Those are already huge improvements over the built-in Angular CLI process. You just need to tweak one thing in the index.html file to enable the service worker.

The service worker registration code is already right there inside the index.html file; you simply need to uncomment it. After that's taken care of, you can kick off a production build.

Building Ionic

In the root directory of the app is a package.json where you can see what options you have for either running the app locally or creating a production-ready bundle. One of the options in there is the npm command ionic:build, which will take care of the production build. Type npm run ionic:build and you have your production-ready files. Unlike the other projects you've looked at in this chapter, Ionic will build your web production files into a *www* directory, like in Figure 11-18.

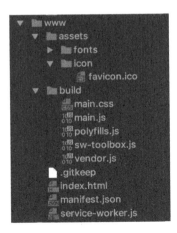

Figure 11-18. *The result of running an Ionic production build, which gives you an app manifest and a service worker*

Note   Remember that Ionic is, first and foremost, a native app solution, so any web-specific builds need a special output directory.

In the www directory, you should have your app manifest and a service-worker.js file. Those files were just copied over from the src directory, which contains an editable service worker file. No need to mess with any configuration files; the service-worker.js is right there. So if you want to add in runtime caching, background syncing, or push notifications, that's your spot.

You can already see that the Ionic team has put in a bit more of a focus on PWAs because you're getting nice support without having to do much of anything, except commenting out the registration code. Now comes the moment of truth: let's deploy the app.

Deploying and Testing the Ionic PWA

This is your last PWA project to deploy, which is good because Firebase limits the number of projects you can have for free. You can find the Ionic PWA you're going to test here: https://ionic-pwa-6d2e5.firebaseapp.com/.

Open it up in the browser and take a look in DevTools. You've got a manifest and a service worker. Moving down to the cache, you can see in Figure 11-19 that pre-caching works by default.

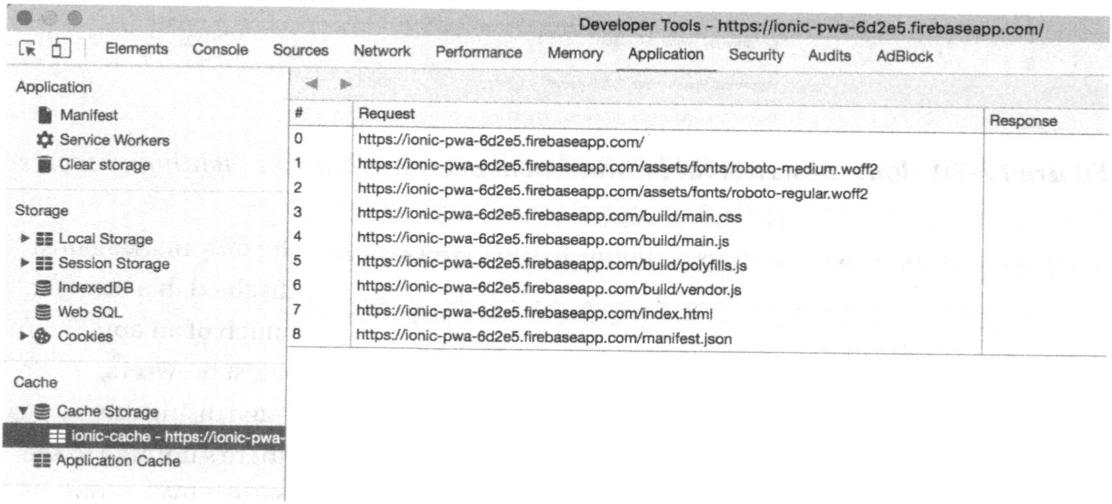

Figure 11-19. Pre-caching works with no configuration

It looks like everything is in order here for a really solid Lighthouse score. Let's take a look at the results in Figure 11-20.

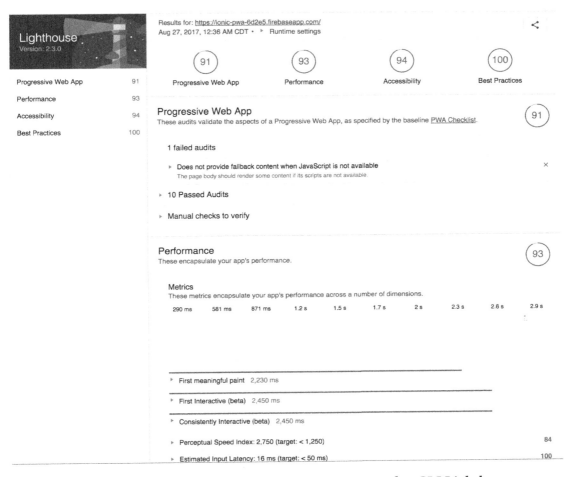

Figure 11-20. *Ionic posts a solid improvement over Angular CLI Lighthouse scores*

Ionic improves on Angular by 27 points in the PWA category. The only mark against Ionic is a lack of anything showing on the page when JavaScript is disabled in a browser. That might seem kind of silly, since without JavaScript, there's not much of an app anyway. But remember the *progressive* part of PWAs. Even on the oldest browsers, the user needs to see *something*. This is a very easily fixed issue, though, using the `<noscript>` tag and putting a string of text in there explaining that there's nothing to see here if the user disabled JavaScript. With that tweak, say hello to a perfect PWA score.

In the Best Practices category, Ionic bests the Angular CLI by 15 points, though there was a drop of a few points in the Accessibility category. It's definitely still an acceptably high score, though.

The interesting score is Performance as it's only a point below Angular's score. So you make huge improvements in two areas while only losing a point on Performance and a few points on Accessibility.

The average Time to First Interactive is only 150 milliseconds slower than Angular. You can see the comparison to other frameworks in Figure 11-21.

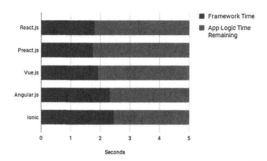

Figure 11-21. *Time to First Interactive across all frameworks and libraries. Ionic's is slowest, but by a marginal amount and with vastly improved PWA and Best Practice scores.*

Ionic takes up about half of the allotted time of your goal, leaving a little more than 2.5 seconds to load your app's resources.

Summary of Ionic's PWA Offering

If you're looking to whip up a quick and simple PWA or an app that has a heavy mobile focus, and you're partial to Angular, then Ionic is undoubtedly a better option. With little to no configuration, you get a near perfect PWA score, a big improvement to Best Practices, with only the slightest drop in performance.

If, on the other hand, you're planning a bigger Angular project, you may be better off manually improving the PWA capabilities of an Angular app.

No matter which route you go, Ionic really improves on Angular CLI from the PWA perspective and is very comparable to the other solutions you've examined.

Starting a PWA from Scratch

What a great time to be a developer focusing on PWAs! Almost any solution you turn to, you should not only have great support for PWAs, but really solid performance as well.

Preact obviously takes home a much deserved overall PWA gold medal and to boot was the easiest setup that provided the most value for your time. But you really can't go wrong with even the poorest performing solution we examined: Angular. Using the skills you've learned throughout this book, you should be able to improve those scores in no time at all, and the performance wasn't far enough away from Preact that you should dismiss it out of hand.

There are still a few other things you can do to squeeze a drop or two of extra performance out of your app.

Looking Ahead

What I'll talk about next isn't necessarily PWA-specific. You've learned just about all there is to know about PWAs. For now. Where you're going, you don't need to know about PWAs.

PART IV

Leveling Up Your PWA

CHAPTER 12

Leveling Up Your PWA

At this point, your official PWA education is complete. Congratulations! Using what you've learned in this book, you now should be able to create a web application that loads fast, is installable on Android devices, works completely offline, and engages users. However, there is always more to learn. Developers tend to be smart people, and smart people are going to keep coming up with better and better ways to do things. That's what this chapter is about: taking steps beyond what you've learned about PWAs and making your apps even better. That will include even more performance patterns and enhancements, like Google's PRPL pattern, lazy loading, code splitting, server-side rendering, and web workers. You'll explore all of that and more in this chapter. If you've made it this far, you've earned enough XP; it's time to level up your PWA!

Google's PRPL Pattern

PRPL is a pattern of best practices to build fast web applications. It was "discovered" by the Polymer team at Google. It's not a technology in and of itself, but a collection of things you can do to make the user's experience in your app a great one. Even better, you've been using most of the PRPL pattern all along, but now you have a name for it.

- **P: Push** resources for the initial route. I've gone over server push quite a few times in our journey here, but again, this is important to eliminate the need for multiple requests from the browser when the server is capable of pushing the resources an initial page needs all at once.

- **R: Render** the initial route. Not just render, but render it fast. Use the app shell architecture to make the first route super-light so the user gets instant content. Sometimes that means using `rel="preload"` or inlining styles or inlining JavaScript or just removing render blocking resources. Under five seconds on a 3G connection, and under three seconds on an LTE connection, are great goals for rendering the initial route.

© Dennis Sheppard 2017
D. Sheppard, *Beginning Progressive Web App Development*, https://doi.org/10.1007/978-1-4842-3090-9_12

- **P: Pre-cache** remaining routes. You saw this with almost every library and framework we looked at. Pre-caching is essential to optimal performance. Any resource the initial route doesn't use, but the rest of the app might need is cached before it's even asked for. This way when the user navigates to the other parts of the app that do need those resources, it's already available in the cache.

- **L: Lazy load** everything the user doesn't need on a page. If a user isn't going to need a CSS file or an image until he or she reaches a certain route, there's no need to load it beforehand. It might seem like pre-caching and lazy loading are opposite strategies, but they really play well together. When a user navigates to a route where the resources weren't loaded in advance, they can be lazy loaded from the service worker's cache, resulting in no additional network calls on a lazy loaded route.

Lazy Loading

The goal of lazy loading is to ensure that your app only loads what is necessary for the route the user is navigating to. This means that instead of a 500KB bundle getting downloaded on initial load, there's a chance that the majority of that bundle never loads at all if the user never navigates to the routes that require loading those resources.

I've gone over those first three principles of PRPL quite a few times, but I haven't discussed lazy loading. One of the reasons for that is that while the concept is simple in theory, the implementation of lazy loading is largely dependent upon whatever framework or library you're using. Additionally, a prerequisite of lazy loading is something called *code splitting*, so let's talk about that next.

Code Splitting

One of the excellent features of HTTP/2 is that requests are fast and cheap. The browser can make dozens of requests at the same time, which causes monolithic bundles to be a sort of anti-pattern. Why would you load 500KB of resources when you only need 5KB for the initial load? This means you can be ultra-smart about how you split up your bundle. Rather than blocking rendering with that huge monolithic chunk, code splitting allows you to download and parse just what you need on a route and pre-cache the rest.

This is significantly different from past JavaScript deployment best practices. Previously, we would minify and concatenate and that's our bundle. The browser downloads it and parses it, and that's just the way it's worked for years. That answer isn't good enough anymore because we have the ability to do better.

You may have noticed one commonality among the libraries and frameworks you played with in the last chapter. Their build processes were all built on Webpack. Webpack is kind of the *de facto* standard of building and bundling front-end applications nowadays. Using Webpack, you're actually able to split your code into multiple bundles that you can load either asynchronously or on demand.

Note   Webpack is not a requirement to implement code splitting. There are other methods by which you can split your code into separate, smaller bundles. As of 2017, however, Webpack is rather ubiquitous in the JavaScript build landscape. In 2018 or 2019, that could change.

The method by which you can do this will once again vary based on your application. After all, Webpack doesn't know where the best place to split your code is unless you help it out a little. While many frameworks and their build systems abstract away the Webpack details (which isn't a bad thing, by the way, since rumors abound about developers getting lost in a Webpack config and never being heard from again), we can still take a look at how you might go about splitting up your code bundle:

```
const path = require('path');
const HTMLWebpackPlugin = require('html-webpack-plugin');

module.exports = {
  entry: {
    popular-movies: './src/popular-movies.js',
    new-movies: './src/new-movies.js'
  },
  output: {
    filename: '[name].bundle.js',
    path: path.resolve(__dirname, 'dist')
  }
};
```

Here you're specifying two different code modules in the `entry` property of Webpack's `module.exports` object. The result of these two modules is two bundles named `popular-movies.bundle.js` and `new-movies.bundle.js`.

If the initial route of the application only needs the `popular-movies` bundle, that's all the initial route requests. You can create multiple small bundles out of your app since HTTP/2 welcomes as many bundles as you can throw at it.

There are various ways to split your code, so depending on the library or framework you're using, do a little bit of research on how to implement code splitting that makes sense for your application. For now, let's move on to additional methods of improving that all-important first page load.

Analyzing Bundles

The bane of a browser's performance focus is giant resources. They take a long time to download, and the browser has to figure out what to do with them. That's one of the reasons that all of your PWAs from scratch loaded so quickly. The bundle sizes of each of them were remarkably small.

Oftentimes throughout the development process of an application, we try out libraries, decide they're not quite what we wanted or needed, and then try another library. Or, we pull in an entire library for one small thing, much like the Movies Finder app is doing with the expansion of the mobile menu. It references the entire jQuery library for one small function.

In either of those cases, the result is a bloated JavaScript bundle. Once your JavaScript resources are bundled, it's difficult to really see what's included in there. Additionally, your `node_modules` folder usually consists of ten pounds of "Nope!" in a five-pound bag. Good luck figuring out what you can pluck out of there. The `package.json` file is better in smaller projects, but as your project grows, so too does your `package.json`.

Thankfully there are solutions to seeing exactly what is in your JavaScript bundles. One such solution is the `webpack-bundle-analyzer` package. The process for using this will vary slightly depending on your setup, but let's take a look at an analysis of the Movies Finder PWA app.

If you still have the Movies Finder code around, go back to that directory, and if not go ahead and re-clone the repo here: `https://github.com/dennissheppard/Movies-Finder`.

Then run `npm install --save-dev webpack-bundle-analyzer -g` to install the npm package.

The next step to analyze Movies Finder's bundles is specific to the Angular CLI, but if you have a non-framework specific webpack.config.js file, you can run webpack --profile --json > stats.json to generate metadata about your bundle that will live in a file called stats.json.

For the Movies Finder app, however, you'll run ng build --prod --stats-json to generate the stats.json file. Then to actually see your bundle analysis, you just need to run webpack-bundle-analyzer dist/stats.json. This command will launch a browser tab where you can visually assess your bundle, as in Figure 12-1.

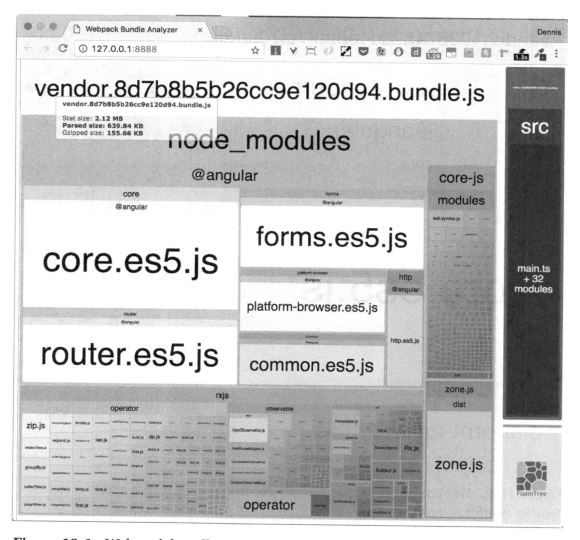

Figure 12-1. *Webpack bundle analyzer is helpful in identifying what's included in your built bundles*

As you can see, there are a lot of items that get put into your bundles. In the case of Movies Finder, the bulk of your app is in the *vendor* bundle. A good portion of that *vendor* bundle is *rxjs*. However, the app doesn't use a large amount of what's included in rxjs.

By comparison, you can go through this same process on the Angular CLI PWA you built in the last chapter. The results for that PWA are in Figure 12-2.

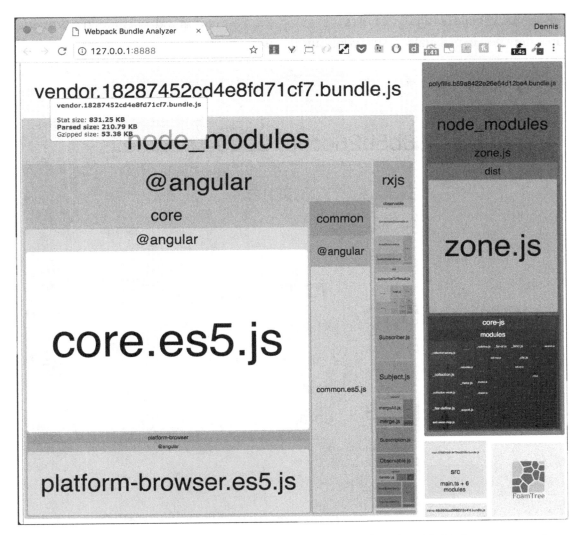

Figure 12-2. *Webpack bundle analyzer for the Angular CLI PWA shows a much smaller vendor bundle*

When you're not importing and using features of libraries, you're going to drastically reduce bundle size. Examining the differences in those two *vendor* bundles shows that by adding in routing, for example, you're increasing your bundle size. This isn't to suggest you shouldn't use routing in your apps, but it does point out that you should be aware of everything you're importing.

A great example of this with the Movies Finder app is that the part of the app that makes API calls imports all of the *rxjs* library, but it only actually *needs* the map operator:

```
// import 'rxjs/Rx';
import 'rxjs/add/operator/map';
```

Making this simple switch in one file of that entire app reduces the *vendor* bundle size from 156KB to 123KB (gzipped). That's a 21% reduction in bundle size by only importing the portion of the library you need instead of the entire library!

Remember, as a general rule, the less code you have to ship to the browser, the faster your app is going to load.

Server-Side Rendering

A long time ago, logic for web apps was all taken care of by the server. Doing anything on the screen, like clicking a button, required a trip to the server to return the entire page again. These were called *postbacks* and in general they resulted in a bad user experience.

As JavaScript pervaded the web app landscape, AJAX solved the issue of postbacks and we now only need a subset of data from the server instead of re-rendering the entire page.

The one good thing about those server-rendered pages, though, was that the first page load was pretty fast. Think about the page load process you've experienced in the apps you've looked at so far that are rendered on the client-side compared to how a traditional server-side—rendered app loads.

Figure 12-3 should give you some idea of how server-side rendering works compared to client-side rendering.

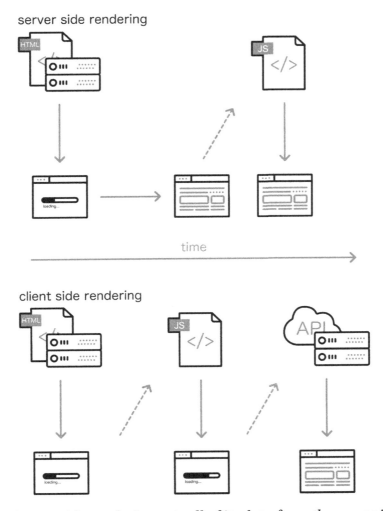

Figure 12-3. *Server-side rendering gets all of its data from the server in one shot, while client-side rendering pulls down the HTML file, requests the JavaScript file, requests data from the API, and then is finally rendered.*

You can actually combine the benefits of server-side rendered pages and client-side rendered pages by only using server-side rendering for the initial page load and sending the JavaScript necessary for page interactivity down after the app shell is visible. Once the JavaScript is downloaded and executed, the page is ready for the user. That process is also called *hydrating* the page.

One of the benefits of this kind of setup, aside from faster loading of initial pages, is SEO. Because the app is fully rendered on the server, search engine crawlers are more easily able to see a full page, improving your search score.

Furthermore, for any users or browsers that may have JavaScript turned off, they would still see an (almost) immediately rendered page, which is a really nice progressive enhancement to have.

You can even pick and choose what you'd like to render on the server. Maybe it makes sense for your application to have the server take care of just the application shell and let the JavaScript take care of the actual content. Because the app shell is loaded almost instantly, the perceived loading time of the app is much quicker for users.

Drawbacks to Server-Side Rendering

All of this sounds great, in theory. The problem that comes along with server-side rendering, however, is complexity. All of your JavaScript code now needs to be able to run on a server as well as in the browser. This is called *Isomorphic* JavaScript, or more recently, *Universal* JavaScript.

Think about how much of your JavaScript code likely references browser-specific objects, like `document` and `window`. None of that exists on the server. You also need to make sure you wrap any DOM manipulation code in a check to insure the server doesn't execute it.

Resources to Implement Server-Side Rendering

In fact, the complexity of Universal JavaScript is such that entire books are written about it, and many frameworks and libraries have separate projects dedicated to server-side rendering. `Next.js` is a very popular framework for server-rendered React applications (and there are many others). `Vue.js` has a project called `Nuxt.js`. *Angular Universal* was a big focus for the Angular team with the new version of Angular.

None of this is to say that you should be scared away from looking into server-side rendering. It makes sense in a lot of cases, but not as much in others. It's another tool at your disposal to try to achieve that ever-elusive 100 Performance score in Lighthouse.

Pre-Rendering

As you're doing additional research on server-side rendering you may run across the term *pre-rendering*. This is the process of taking your initial route and creating a static web page from it. There are build tools that can do this, so that once you have your page pre-rendered, you can distribute it to CDNs. Because the initial route is now a static page, the browser only needs to pull down the HTML and CSS, resulting in what should be a very quickly loading page. The JavaScript needed to "hydrate" the page for any user interactivity can come down separately, avoiding any render blocking.

Let's move on to another rendering problem that JavaScript and the Web has long been faced with, and the solution that will further improve your app's performance.

Web Workers

One of the drawbacks of client-side development is that all code runs on the UI thread. So anything that requires a lot of processing can block the UI from rendering or being interactive. You've likely experienced this with apps that appear to be frozen. For example, take a look at this Plnkr at `http://bit.ly/2wgCOoH`.

Here is the markup:

```
<body>
    <div>
      <div style="padding: 15px;">
        <button id="freezeBtn" onclick="freeze()">
        Freeze Everything!
        </button>
      </div>
    </div>
    <div>
      <img src="https://usatthebiglead.files.wordpress.com/2015/02/dog.gif">
    </div>
    <div>
      <img src="https://media.giphy.com/media/gZLl9szOpgbpS/giphy.gif">
    </div>
</body>
```

And the very important processing going on in the background:

```
function freeze() {
  for (let i = 0; i < 500000; i++) {
    let result = i * i;
    console.log(result);
  }
}
```

When you run this, yes, it appears that there are two adorable dog gifs, and while you're goofily smiling at them, click that button that says *Freeze Everything!* and see what happens. The dogs stopped moving! Why would anyone ever want those dogs to stop doing the cute things they're doing?

Unfortunately they become temporarily frozen because that button kicks off a function that requires intense processing. It's a pointless process in this case, but that's not the point. You've asked the browser to do some kind of processing that is intensive enough that it can no longer properly render the UI. Everything freezes. Rendering, downloading additional resources, parsing other code. Everything. That's a problem if you have anything you need to process on the front end.

You might think that you don't have much you actually need to process on the client side. After all, most processing should happen on the server, right? You're not thinking in terms of this new world of apps on the Web that are as powerful as native apps. For example, there are now web-based spreadsheets. Think about that. If you have a formula in a spreadsheet that calculates hundreds or thousands of numbers, you're not going to want to throw up a loading message every time. Especially a loading message that won't even animate because the entire UI is now unresponsive. There are also web-based games, web-based video, and image processing apps. More and more processing is getting pushed to the browser, and users expect the UI to remain responsive. As they should! So what is a processing-happy, front-end developer to do?

Web workers are the solution. They allow you spin off a collection of work to a script that runs in the background, which is also able to notify the main execution thread when it's finished. Web workers are a multi-threaded JavaScript solution. You can see in Figure 12-4 that the interaction between the JavaScript file and the web worker is the same as with service workers.

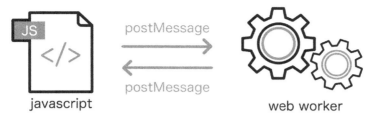

Figure 12-4. *Web workers allow the main UI thread to offload processing to a script that runs in the background, making sure that the UI remains responsive*

Let's take the same code from the gif example in the Plnkr and throw the processing into a web worker. You can see the final result at `http://bit.ly/2wHyVdk`.

The `script.js` from before is now:

```
function freeze() {
  createWorker();
}

function createWorker() {
  var worker = new Worker('worker.js');
  worker.postMessage('start-freeze');

  worker.onmessage = function (e) {
    alert('final number: ' + e.data);
  };
}
```

Instead of doing any processing in here, you now have a `createWorker` function that creates a new `Worker` object, and you pass it your worker script. All of your processing will be done in there by a file called `worker.js`. You can communicate with the worker via *messages*, similar to how you did before with service workers, passing in data if the main thread needs to send the worker any information.

Note   The `postMessage` method requires that you pass *something* in, so you have a string passed in there, even though the worker doesn't actually use it.

The main thread also can listen for a message with `worker.onmessage`, in which data from the worker comes through on the `data` property on the e (event) object.

Moving over to the worker implementation:

```
self.addEventListener('message', function(e) {
  freeze();
});

function freeze() {
  let result;
  for (let i = 1; i < 30000000; i++) {
    result = i * i;
  }
  self.postMessage(result);
}
```

The worker listens for a message. In this case, you just want the worker to start the freeze function. It does, goes through the meaningless loop, and sends the result back to the main thread via the self.postMessage method.

When you run this, not only do you see that the gifs continue animating, but the result is returned significantly faster when the dedicated thread is responsible for calculating it.

You could also configure your worker to make API calls and process the results. Just like you imported the pirate-manager.js app into your service worker before, web workers can also use the importScripts function. If you expect a large amount of data from an API call and you need to process that data, simply import whatever script would typically make the call and call that function from within the web worker. When the call is finished, you can use the messaging mechanism to let the main thread know that the worker has fetched and processed the data.

The cute dog gifs example shows the use of a *dedicated* web worker. The life cycle of this worker is the same as the page that created it. When that page is no longer in scope, the worker dies along with it. If you need a worker to live across multiple pages, you can use a *shared* worker. The instantiation is the same: you just use the SharedWorker constructor when creating your worker rather than just Worker.

Obviously the pointless loop is a vastly simplified example, but you can imagine the power web workers bring to front-end web development. As a bonus, dedicated web workers share universal support across browsers, including mobile Safari. Shared web workers, on the other hand, don't have quite the same level of acceptance, with only Chrome, Firefox, and Opera supporting them.

PWA News

We've had such a great time on this journey of learning everything there is to know about Progressive Web Apps that it inspired some exciting new PWA updates from Apple and Google. Let's see what they've got for us.

Safari

Service worker support is coming to Safari! This is FANTASTIC news! As of early August 2017, Webkit, which is the engine that powers Safari, changed the status of service workers to "in development." Since mobile Safari accounts for a significant share of web traffic, this makes your PWA knowledge all the more important. It's unclear when this will actually be widely available, but Safari Tech Preview 38 has them enabled as an experimental feature. So as a new PWA developer, you now have a responsibility to get out there and fill up the iOS world with service worker and PWA goodness.

Workbox

While you were busy learning, the Google Chrome team released a new service worker generation tool called *Workbox*. It's a collection of libraries and tools to generate a service worker for you, much like how `sw-precache` does.

Before you panic about the possibility of everything you've learned being wasted, don't. Workbox is just another tool in your belt. `sw-precache` is still the default out-of-the-box solution right now for all of the frameworks and libraries you've looked at. Plus, I'll go over what Workbox has to offer. The concepts are all the same, just wrapped up in a new package.

To get started with Workbox, you install it by running `npm install workbox-cli --global`. In the root of your project (feel free to use any of the projects you've gone over throughout the book, or spin up a new project), you can generate a service worker with the following command: `workbox generate:sw`. The CLI will ask you a number of questions, like in Figure 12-5.

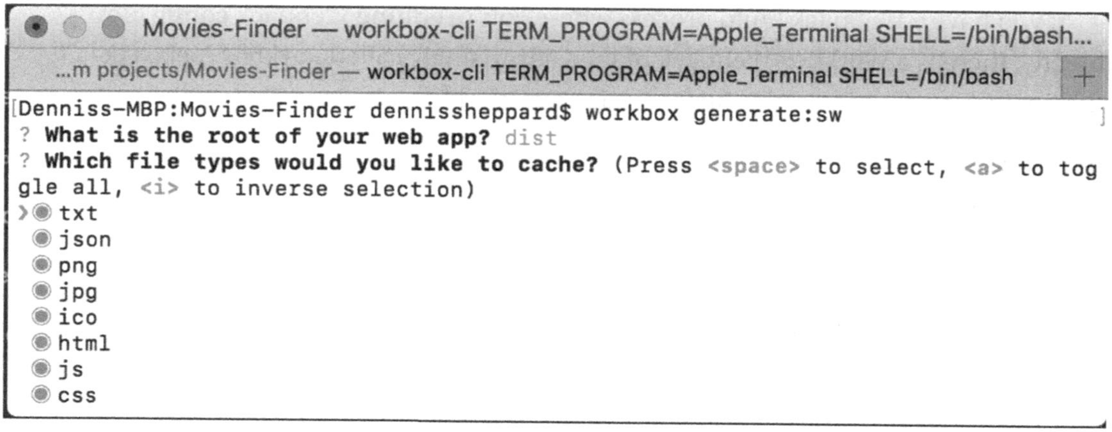

```
●  ●  ●    Movies-Finder — workbox-cli TERM_PROGRAM=Apple_Terminal SHELL=/bin/bash...

...m projects/Movies-Finder — workbox-cli TERM_PROGRAM=Apple_Terminal SHELL=/bin/bash      +

[Denniss-MBP:Movies-Finder dennissheppard$ workbox generate:sw                      ]
? What is the root of your web app? dist
? Which file types would you like to cache? (Press <space> to select, <a> to tog
gle all, <i> to inverse selection)
>◉ txt
 ◉ json
 ◉ png
 ◉ jpg
 ◉ ico
 ◉ html
 ◉ js
 ◉ css
```

Figure 12-5. *Workbox CLI setup*

After those questions, such as what you would like to cache and where you want the CLI to put the resulting service worker, you will have a generated file. If you look in there, you'll see that the result is actually similar to a sw-precache-generated service worker, just with much less code. There's an array of all the files you want to cache, and then at the bottom of the file you see two simple lines tying everything together:

```
const workboxSW = new self.WorkboxSW();
workboxSW.precache(fileManifest);
```

With this, you now have a service worker with pre-caching all set up. You might remember that Workbox is a collection of libraries and tools. *WorkboxSW* is the high-level wrapper that ties all of the modules together. For pre-caching and runtime caching, *WorkboxSW* is likely all you'll ever need. You create a new instance of it and call precache and you're all set.

The result of this generated file is just like every other service worker you've seen, with the same registration process and the same lifecycle. If you like this type of CLI generation, it's easy to plug it into your existing npm build process in the scripts array inside of your package.json, just like you did with the Movies Finder app:

```
"build-sw": "ng build --prod && workbox-cli generate:sw"
```

Note   If you're not using Angular for your PWA project, just replace ng build with whatever your build script happens to be.

If you have a Webpack build process where you're editing Webpack config files directly, there is a Workbox Webpack plugin, surprisingly called workbox-webpack-plugin. In your plugins array, just include your Workbox configuration:

```
plugins: [
    new workboxPlugin({
      globDirectory: '/dist',
      globPatterns: ['**/*.{html,js,css}'],
      swDest: path.join('/dist', 'service-worker.js'),
    }),
  ]
```

Workbox supports runtime caching as well via the router.registerRoute method. The syntax is very similar to using sw-toolbox:

```
workboxSW.router.registerRoute(
  'https://api.themoviedb.org/*',
  workboxSW.strategies.cacheFirst({
    cacheName: 'movies',
    cacheExpiration: {
      maxEntries: 20,
      maxAgeSeconds: 7 * 24 * 60 * 60,
    }
  })
);
```

As you can see, not all that much changed regarding what I've discussed with sw-precache and sw-toolbox compared with Workbox. Instead of having two libraries handling different features, everything is rolled into one.

Try Workbox out on your project and see if you like it. Whether you do or not, for now sw-precache and sw-toolbox are still excellent choices to take care of your caching needs.

A Last Word

Even in the process of writing this book, and certainly while you were reading it, the development landscape morphed. New libraries were released, older ones lost some users, and syntax changed. That's what technology does, and as developers we have to learn to embrace that. It is extremely likely that code you write today will be obsolete in just a few years, and the framework or library you used on that project has a finite lifespan.

However, every **concept** you learned in this book will be relevant as long as the Web continues to dominate in terms of user reach. The syntax will change, browser support might get better (or a new browser might arrive on the scene), and the libraries and frameworks we looked at will come and go. In the end, though, the **principles** that make a Progressive Web App a progressive web app are that it loads fast, it works (even if only minimally) on all browsers, it's reliable with or without an Internet connection, and it engages users in ways that only native applications did in the past. Even as technology changes, those tenets will live far beyond any hot development trend.

The Web is constantly challenged on multiple fronts, and time and again the Web has kept pace or surpassed those challengers. With PWAs, the Web is well equipped to do so once again.

Thanks for reading! Hopefully it was as enjoyable to read and follow along as it was to write. Best of luck!

Index

Get the eBook for only $5!

Why limit yourself?

With most of our titles available in both PDF and ePUB format, you can access your content wherever and however you wish—on your PC, phone, tablet, or reader.

Since you've purchased this print book, we are happy to offer you the eBook for just $5.

To learn more, go to http://www.apress.com/companion or contact support@apress.com.

Apress®

Printed in the United States
By Bookmasters